In the Footsteps of Christ

Faith-Sharing Sessions for Season Three of ARISE Together in Christ

RENEW International
1232 George Street
Plainfield, NJ 07062-1717
www.renewintl.org

Nihil Obstat
Reverend Monsignor James M. Cafone, S.T.D.
Archdiocese of Newark
Censor Librorum

Imprimatur
Most Reverend John J. Myers, J.C.D., D.D.
Archbishop of Newark

Cover design by Robert B. Kelly
Book design by Linda L. Eberly and Robert B. Kelly

ISBN: 1-930978-63-4

Printed and bound in the United States of America

TABLE OF CONTENTS

ACKNOWLEDGMENTS

We gratefully acknowledge the use of the following quotations:

on page viii, Pius X as quoted by Dom Jean-Baptiste Chautard, O.C.S.O., in *The Soul of the Apostolate* (translated into English by Thomas Merton)

on pages 11, 19-20, 39, 57 from the *New Revised Standard Version Bible* (containing the Old and New Testaments with the Apocryphal/Deuterocanonical Books) © 1989 by the Division of Christian Education of the National Council of the Churches of Christ in the U.S.A., and are used by permission. All rights reserved.

on page 14, from *Called and Gifted* (Reflections of the U.S. Catholic Bishops on the 30th Anniversary of the *Decree on the Apostolate of the Laity* and the 15th Anniversary of *Called and Gifted*), © 1995, United States Catholic Conference, Inc., (Washington, D.C.)

on page 21, from the *Rite of Ordination of Deacons*, English translation © International Committee on English in the Liturgy, Inc. (ICEL)

on page 21, from *Befriending the Stranger* by Jean Vanier (Darton, Longman & Todd, 2005)

on page 22, prayer (adapted) from prayers for the laity, *Roman Missal*. English translation © 1973 ICEL

on pages 23-25, from *Scenes from a Parish: RENEW Faith-Sharing Edition* (DVD, plus Guide in English, plus Guía en español)

on page 28 from *Sharing Catholic Social Teaching: Challenges and Directions*, © 1998 United States Catholic Conference, Inc., (Washington, D.C.)

on page 32, prayer (adapted) from Instruction and Prayer over the people, *Rite of Confirmation* (Second edition). English translation © ICEL

on pages 33, 67 from the English translation of the *Catechism of the Catholic Church for the United States of America* Copyright © 1994, United States Conference of Catholic Bishops—Libreria Editrice Vaticana. English translation of the *Catechism of the Catholic Church: Modifications from the Editio Typica* Copyright © 1997, United States Conference of Catholic Bishops—Libreria Editrice Vaticana. Used with permission.

on page 38, from "Meditation XVII" by John Donne (1572-1631) in *Devotions Upon Emergent Occasions* (published 1624)

on pages 34-36, from the letter of Sister Ita Ford. *"Here I Am, Lord": The Letters and Writings of Ita Ford* by Ita Ford and Jeanne Evans (Orbis Books, 2005)

on page 45, from *The Two Gentlemen of Verona* by William Shakespeare (1564-1616)

on page 45, from *Sacred Dwelling: A Spirituality of Family Life*, © 2007 Wendy M. Wright. Originally published by Darton, Longman and Todd (London); first U.S. edition by Pauline Books and Media/ Daughters of St. Paul (Boston, MA). Used by permission of Pauline Books & Media, 50 St. Paul's Ave, Boston, MA 02130. All rights reserved.

on page 46, prayer (adapted) from *Catholic Household Blessings and Prayers* (Revised edition) © 2007 USCCB Committee on Liturgy

pages 49-53 are based on *Follow the Way of Love*, Pastoral Message of the U.S. Bishops © 1994, United States Catholic Conference, Inc., Washington, D.C.

on page 56, from the final blessing (adapted), *Rite of Marriage*. English translation © ICEL

on page 58, prayer for solidarity from *Being Neighbor: the Catechism and Social Justice*, CCHD/USCCB, © 2003 United States Catholic Conference, Inc., Washington, D.C.

on pages 60, from *Economic Justice for All*, Pastoral Letter of the U.S. Catholic Bishops on Catholic Social Teaching and the U.S. Economy © 1986 United States Catholic Conference, Inc., Washington, D.C.

on page 63, from *Strength to Love* by Martin Luther King, Jr., (Fortress Press, 1981)

on pages 63-64, from *Communities of Salt and Light: Reflections on the Social Mission of the Parish*, developed by the Domestic Social Policy Committee and the International Policy Committee of the USCCB, and approved by the Catholic Bishop of the United States as a statement of the USCCB © 1994, United States Catholic Conference, Inc., Washington, D.C.

on page 67, "Lord, try us" by Helder Camara, in *The Desert Is Fertile*, English translation by Dinah Livingston © 1974 Orbis Books

on page 68, opening prayer for the First Sunday of Advent, *Roman Missal* English translation © 1973 ICEL

on page 69, from 'Priesthood in the Service of Justice" in *Priests for the New Millennium* © 2000, United States Catholic Conference, Inc., Washington, D.C.

on pages 77-79, the complete text of *Key Themes of Catholic Social Teaching*, by the U.S. Catholic Bishops, © 2005, United States Catholic Conference, Inc., Washington, D.C.

All of the papal and conciliar documents quoted in this book are from the English translations as presented by the Vatican website.

Presenting RENEW International

ARISE Together in Christ is a three-year process of evangelization and spiritual renewal developed by RENEW International. The ***ARISE*** process is one of the most recent among those that RENEW International offers.

The RENEW process, both parish-based and diocesan-wide, was first developed and implemented in the Archdiocese of Newark, New Jersey. Its success there led other dioceses, in the United States, and in other countries, to bring RENEW to their people and parish communities. In the three decades since its vibrant beginnings, RENEW International has touched the lives of 25 million people in over 150 dioceses in the United States and 23 countries throughout the world.

RENEW International has grown organically from its original single RENEW process. Materials and training have been inculturated and made available in over 40 languages. We have added specific pastoral outreach to campuses, and to young adults in their 20s and 30s. We have incorporated prison ministry, and provided resources for the visually impaired.

The very core of all of these processes remains the same: to help people become better hearers and doers of the Word of God. We do this by encouraging and supporting the formation of small communities who gather prayerfully to reflect on and share the Word of God, to make better connections between faith and life, and to live their faith more concretely in family, work, and community life.

As a not-for-profit organization, our pastoral outreach is sustained in part from the sales of our publications and resources, and the stipends we receive for the services provided to parishes and dioceses. However, our priority is always to serve all parishes who desire to renew their faith and build the Church, regardless of their economic situation. We have been able to fulfill this mission not only in the inner city and rural areas in the United States, but also in the developing world, especially Latin America and Africa, thanks to donations and charitable funding.

As you meet in your small group, we invite you to take a few moments to imagine the great invisible network of others, here in the United States and on the other continents. They gather, as you do, in small Christian communities, around the Word of God present in the Scripture, striving to hear and act upon that Word. Keep them in your prayer: a prayer of thanksgiving for the many graces we have experienced; a prayer that the Spirit will guide all of us so that we become evermore "together in Christ."

Introduction

ARISE has led us to explore the meaning and power of our encounter with Christ (Season One), and our need to foster that relationship through ongoing, life-long conversion (Season Two).

Season Three of ***ARISE*** faces a fundamental aspect of Christian life, as we explore what it means to walk "in the footsteps of Christ." We will focus on some of the key themes of Catholic social teaching, and in particular the commitment this implies to acts of charity and works of justice. There is a sense in which the Invitation to Act element of our sessions might seem to assume a greater importance.

However, it is important to realize how all of what we explore this Season is itself founded on the first two Seasons. First and foremost, to remember it is Christ who gives meaning to our lives as Christians. Our encounter with Christ in baptism is not a past event; it is the beginning of a dynamic, living, and life-giving personal relationship. This is a relationship that needs to be nourished by our making a place for him in lives: seeking Christ in the Word; being led by him into prayer to the Father, both in the liturgy (the Mass and the other sacraments), and in our personal prayer. It is this Spirit-filled interior life that can empower, in Christ, everything we do in life.

The very nature of our ***ARISE*** meetings is meant to foster that full sense of life in faith. We do not meet together simply to pray. However, we gather and consciously remember Christ's presence, so that all we do together is done prayerfully, that is, in a way that opens our hearts and minds to God. We do not meet together simply to study Scripture. But Scripture is central to this time together, as we break open the Word, seeing ourselves as members in a chain that links us across time to the evangelists and other sacred writers, seeking, through the eyes of faith, to see God in our lives. We do not meet together simply to plan and commit to good actions. But we accept the challenge of an authentic faith that implies commitment to building a better world, better relationships among ourselves.

The real secret is not in any one of these elements, but in their delicate interrelationship and balance, in the way that leaves us open to the Spirit. The mission of the Church, and so being a Christian, is fulfilled in prayer and action, both rooted in and flowing from the Word of God.

In this Season of ***ARISE*** we are going to explore what it means to walk "in the footsteps of Christ." Just about 100 years ago, at a very tumultuous time in history, Pius X reflected on exactly this–what today we might call our "mission" as Christians–except the word he used was "apostolate." His perceptive comments, warning yet encouragement, have lost none of their force nor appropriateness:

> "Without interior life we will never have the strength to persevere in sustaining all the difficulties inseparable from any apostolate: the coldness and lack of cooperation even on the part of the virtuous; the calumnies of our adversaries; and at times even the jealousy of friends and comrades in arms ... only a patient virtue, unshakably based upon the good, and at the same time smooth and tactful, is able to move these difficulties to one side and diminish their power."

May the Spirit of Christ keep us true to his Word as we explore how we are called to make present the Good News here and now in our communities.

Faith Sharing in a Small Community

Welcome to the third Season of ***ARISE Together in Christ.***

Some of you have already experienced meeting and sharing in small communities. For others, this may be a new experience.

You are coming together as a group, but you are not just meeting together as a discussion or study group where you talk about ideas. Rather, you gather in small Christian communities as a sharing group, open to the Spirit of God, seeking to grow in faith and in your relationship with God, and one another.

For all of you engaging in this spiritual adventure together, here are some key ideas that help bring about good, healthy faith sharing.

Gathering

The first fundamental is that you have chosen to gather as a small community to share prayer, life, and faith in a way that will enrich your own lives, the life of your parish community, and the life of the diocese as a community. The members of the small group need to take the time to get to know one another. Always allow time for introductions at the first session. Then, at later sessions, take a moment or two to ask each other how you are and what has happened since you last met. If anyone new joins the group, again allow time for introductions. The goal is to form a community.

Hospitality and Environment

The right atmosphere is very important for faith sharing. The members of the group need to feel comfortable, physically and psychologically. Effective sharing needs a reflective atmosphere, with as few distractions as possible. It is good to establish a central focus, using something that will help direct thoughts toward the theme of the session.

During this Season we explore what it means to walk "in the footsteps of Christ." The metaphor of journey implied by this title could be evoked by a picture of a road open before us (sample available for download from the online ***ARISE*** library). A central question throughout this Season, especially as we think of our commitment to action is: how will we show we are truly disciples of Christ? The prophetic call from Micah 6, printed out as a poster, could serve as a focal point (again, a sample is available from the online ***ARISE*** library). The Scripture for session five is the parable of the Good Samaritan; this is one of the most illustrated episodes from the Gospels, so you should be able to find an image in a style of art that matches the spiritual sensibilities of your group. The concluding session proposes a ritual of light, with each participant taking home a candle; you might think of putting an appropriate symbol on this personal candle. For example, the ***ARISE*** sunburst symbol printed on transparent labels could then be applied to glass tea-light candle holders. For any session it would be extremely appropriate to have a Bible, open at the key passage for the session: this emphasizes the central role that the Word of God has in guiding our sharing.

Timing

It is very important to get the timing of the session right. Under usual circumstances, a session should last 90 minutes. Most groups then extend their time together in a brief social. The time together in the session should have a balance of prayer, talking about our own experience, exploring Scripture, reflection, faith sharing, and talking about ways of living out our faith. This balance is presented in more detail on pages 8-10.

Prayer

Prayer can, and should take different forms. Invite different members of the group to lead the moments of prayer. Do not forget that silence is a very important part of any prayer, so build moments of quiet into the time of prayer, with a gentle but explicit prompt from whoever is leading the prayer. For example:

> Let us spend a few moments in quiet,
> becoming more aware of God's presence ...
> ... God's presence in each one of us,
> and especially in this community,
> gathered in Jesus' name.

Songs are suggested for the moments of prayer, and all of the songs listed in this book can be found on the *In the Footsteps of Christ CD.* However, these are only suggestions. If you can think of a more appropriate song, then you should substitute that for what we propose.

Experience

Our spiritual lives do not exist without us! Our experience, then, is essential to our spiritual lives. We need to reflect on our story—what we have experienced in our families, in our other relationships—and explore how that relates to the theme of the session. You will notice that the ***Breaking Open Our Story*** reflections this book offers are usually expressed in the first person. This is not just because they are stories that someone really did share with us. This use of the first person is also designed as a model for sharing, as an explicit encouragement to all of us to dare to say "I remember ..." and then to interpret that experience through the eyes of faith.

Scripture

Others before us read their experiences through the eyes of faith, and in it saw the great story of God's loving relationship with his people. This is set out in what we call the Scriptures, the story God reveals to us, most of all through Christ his Son, the eternal Word. The faith-sharing session gives prominence to ***Breaking Open God's Story***, exploring Scripture, noticing what word, phrase, or image from it speaks to us. In a word, we share how it has touched our hearts. We are offered input to help us understand what God is saying to us today. Then we reflect together on our experience, our story and God's story—and above all how the two link together. All are invited to reflect: each person who wishes to share his or her reflection aloud is given the opportunity to do so. No one dominates, and no one need talk unless he or she wants to.

Challenge and Commitment

One of the key components of faith sharing is how we take what we hear and share, and live it out in our lives. That is why a moment of challenge is built into every session. We are given the opportunity to respond, not just verbally, but by making a commitment to a clear and specific action that we see as a consequence of living out the faith expressed in the sharing. At the following meeting, we are invited to share how we did at living out that commitment.

We live in a hectic, busy world. Making time for outreach or action will not always be easy. The importance of this moment is the opportunity it gives us to reassess our priorities. The key question is not so much "Did I do what I said I would?" but rather "Through this activity, did I manage to live out my faith?" This should also make us look to the bigger question of living out our faith in the totality of our lives: in our family, in our other relationships, in our work environment. We may discover that rather than doing "more" it might be more important for us to do "less"! This is the time to look at how we are living the values of Jesus and the Gospel, and to identify what needs to change in our behaviors and attitudes.

The Role of the Leader

Each small community will have its leader. In a faith-sharing context, the leader is not someone with all the answers who is there to preach or teach. The leader is a participant, with the particular responsibility of helping the group by

- doing whatever is necessary to prepare for each session. It certainly involves reading over the session in advance, so as to be totally at home with the focus, reflection, and questions. Preparing could also include delegating people to prepare the readings that will be used in the session; delegating the person who will lead the prayer; arranging and/or delegating others to plan and arrange the environment.
- guiding the group through the faith-sharing process. Gently keeping the sharing focused on the theme of the session. Moving the sharing from one moment to another, so that the balance and overall timing is respected.
- listening, and being prepared to ask questions that will keep the faith sharing moving yet focused.
- ensuring that every participant who wants to speak has the opportunity to do so.

More detailed suggestions for the leader are included in *Sowing Seeds: Essentials for Small Community Leaders,* which is part of the ***ARISE*** Parish Kit (for more details, see page 84).

Faith-Sharing Principles and Guidelines

The following Guidelines will keep your faith-sharing community focused, and help you to grow in faith, hope, and love.

Principles

- Faith is a gift from God. God leads each person on his or her spiritual journey. This happens in the context of the Christian community.
- Christ, the Word made flesh, is the root and foundation of Christian faith. It is because of Christ, and in and through him that we come together to share our faith.
- "Faith sharing" refers to the shared reflections on the action of God in one's life experience as related to Scripture and the faith of the Church.
- Faith sharing is not discussion, problem solving, nor Scripture study. It is an opportunity for an encounter between a person in the concrete circumstances of his or her own life and a loving God, leading to a conversion of heart.
- The entire faith-sharing process is an expression of prayerful reflection.

Guidelines

- Constant attention to respect, honesty, and openness for each person will assist the community's growth.
- Each person shares on the level where he or she feels comfortable.

- Silence is a vital part of the total process. Participants are given time to reflect before any sharing begins, and a period of comfortable silence might occur between sharing by individual participants.
- Before sharing a second time, participants are encouraged to wait until all others who wish to do so have contributed.
- The entire community is responsible for participating and faith sharing.
- Confidentiality, allowing each person to share honestly, is essential.
- The natural culmination of the sharing should be the action commitment, the key to the spiritual growth of both individuals and community.

The Structure and Flow of a Session

On pages 1-5, we presented some of the key elements that should be present for good, healthy faith sharing. We also talked about the importance of a balance. Here is another way of looking at a session, paying attention to the way it should be structured so that there is a natural flow, one part leading the participants to the next, deeper stage.

Having a structured routine frees the group from having to figure out "What do we do next?" It allows the members to concentrate on the what, rather than the how, to pay more attention to their inner selves and to the Word of God.

If you follow the suggested timings, then a session will last 90 minutes.

GATHER (Step 1) *[15 minutes]*

Elements

- Introductions *[First time only]*
- Opening Prayer *[5 minutes]*
- Living Our Faith *[10 minutes]*
- Focus

Purpose

- This is a sacred time. We enter it deliberately, as a community who have chosen to faith share together.
- We greet each other, we consciously put ourselves in the presence of God and we pray for the grace to grow in faith.

- We share how the previous session has influenced our lives since we last met.
- We focus on the theme of the session that is about to unfold.

[15 minutes]

BREAKING OPEN OUR STORY (Step 2)

Elements

- Reflection, based on experience *[5 minutes]*
- A question, or two *[10 minutes]*

Purpose

- This part is about "my story," and how it relates to the theme of the session, what it says about my relationships (family, friends, work).
- After listening to a short reflection, everyone has the opportunity—helped by the questions—to reflect upon and share something of their own experience.

[40 minutes]

BREAKING OPEN GOD'S STORY (Step 3)

Elements

- Scripture Reading *[5 minutes]*
- Moment of reflection and brief sharing, prompted by the Scripture Reading *[5 minutes]*
- A reflection *[10 minutes]*
- Three questions to prompt sharing *[20 minutes]*

Purpose

- This part is about exploring "God's story" and in particular how it is speaking to us today.
- The short reflection helps us deepen our understanding of the Scripture text.
- The questions are designed to prompt sharing, which breaks open the Word of God in a way that changes heads, hearts, and hands. Heads: hopefully we may come to a new or deeper understanding of the passage. Hearts: this fresh or renewed understanding prompts a change of attitude on our part. Hands: to what action are we challenged by this?

INVITATION TO ACT (Step 4) *[20 minutes]*

Elements

- Commitment to an action, and suggestions for actions *[15 minutes]*
- Closing prayer *[5 minutes]*

Purpose

- This part prompts the participants to understand that faith and faith sharing should impel us to commit to a specific and concrete act in the coming week, which flows from the sharing. This may be either a personal or a group action. Above all, it should be an action that, while challenging, is eminently doable.
- Suggestions, linked to the theme of the reflection, are offered by this book. These are secondary to actions that the group members themselves discern as the fruit of their sharing.
- The faith-sharing session concludes—as it began—in prayer.

Called to Follow in Christ's Footsteps

"Where two or three are gathered in my name, I am there among them."

Matthew 18:20

"Stay with us, Lord!"

Cf. Luke 24:29

Focus for this Session

- Seeing life's journey through the eyes of faith
- Christ walks with us
- Using our gifts for the good of the community
- Journey with Christ to "Jerusalem"

GATHER

Introductions

Allow a few moments for everyone to share a little about their life since the end of Season Two. For those joining the group for the first time, allow them a few moments to introduce themselves, and to share how they became interested in joining the ***ARISE Together in Christ*** *process.*

Opening Prayer

Leader As we gather for our first meeting
of Season Three of ***ARISE Together in Christ,***
let us spend a moment of quiet
in order to become more aware of God's presence ...
... God's presence in each of us
and in the community.

One of the members reads the following prayer:

Good and gracious God,
you accompany us with love
as we journey through life.
You sent us your Son, to share our journey.
He is the way that leads us back to you,
the truth that sets us free,
the life that makes our joy complete.
May your Spirit be with us today,
and in the weeks ahead,
as we open our hearts and minds
to what this journey means.
Strengthen us as we strive
to put our faith into action,
and so bring others to know
the companionship of Christ.
We ask this in the name of Jesus the Lord.

All **Amen.**

Suggested Song
Christ Be Beside Me

BREAKING OPEN OUR STORY

Reflection

In Season One of ***ARISE Together in Christ***, we embarked on an extraordinary journey together, seeking a deeper encounter with Jesus the Christ. Our companions and guides were Mark, Matthew, Luke, John, and Paul. Above all, we explored how because of our Baptism we are now living a new life, the life of the Risen Christ in the community of the Church.

In Season Two we explored the theme of "conversion." Conversion means turning life around; turning away from an old life and turning toward a new life in God. Again, we saw this as a consequence of our Baptism, as being the beginning of a lifelong process of becoming fully who we already are—children of God.

Now in Season Three of ***ARISE Together in Christ***, we will explore together yet another consequence of our Baptism: what it means both personally and as a community, to walk in the footsteps of Christ as we face today's challenges and opportunities.

A good friend of mine is a national speaker in the area of catechesis. She once shared with me her memories of her first public appearances. "I was suffering from panic attacks, couldn't sleep or eat the day before my presentation," she said, adding, "I always feared that I was going to make mistakes or even faint." I thought she was exaggerating, because when I saw her delivering a major address to a crowd of more than 1,000 people, she looked so confident and in control.

Several years later, when I met her again at a national conference, her presentation seemed different. She still looked sure of herself and delivered a wonderful speech, but I saw humility in her that I had never seen before. Over lunch afterwards, I asked her about this.

She told me that she had finally shared her anxiety about public speaking with her spiritual companion, who then guided her through a self-evaluation process. Part of this process was to acknowledge her talent and gift for public-speaking. It also meant recognizing that she had been planning her presentations as if everything depended on her talents alone.

This turned her around. Now she saw in a new way her natural gifts as God-given and so as an invitation from God to use them for the benefit of others. Her focus shifted away from herself and onto the good not just that she could do, but that she should do. She let her natural talents, learned skills, and professional training be enhanced and enriched by the power of the Spirit of the risen Christ.

My friend became aware that when she tried to journey alone and relied solely on herself, anxiety would creep in. When she thought of Jesus walking with her, she was at peace, reassured. Now before beginning a presentation, she thinks of Christ being present, alongside her, and so she prays: "Jesus, you sent me to do this task. Take the gifts you have given me and use them for the benefit of the people present here today. Don't let me become an obstacle to your message of Good News."

Prayer and action now work harmoniously in her life. In fact, her action is now prayer in a very real sense: something offered to God and for others. "Holiness" is not about turning away from this world (see sidebar). It is about journeying through this world, seeing it through the eyes of faith, and, in the footsteps of Christ, dispelling anxiety and building joy and hope not just for ourselves, but above all for others.

Three key challenges

"Because the laity's call to holiness is a vocation in every sense of the word, it makes demands and poses challenges. Many challenges are embedded in the call to holiness …, but we have raised up three as particularly apt for our time:

(1) to make an explicit connection between holiness and active service, especially to the poor and vulnerable;

(2) to recognize that human suffering—so much a part of the laity's life—can be the catalyst for them to carry forth the Church's healing ministry in diverse ways;

(3) to reappropriate the Church's tradition of a simple lifestyle in light of the pressing need for justice, as well as preserving the earth for ourselves and for generations to come.

The laity's call to holiness is a gift from the Holy Spirit. Their response is a gift to the Church and to the world."

USCCB, *Called and Gifted for the Third Millennium*

Invitation to Share

Take a few moments of silence to reflect on one of the following questions. Then share your reflections.

1. What natural talents or learned skills do you use in service to your parish or broader community? Are there gifts which you sense you may not yet have fully embraced?
2. What might change in the way you do ordinary things if you thought that Christ was alongside you? In what ways would this be a consoling presence? In what ways would it be a challenging presence?

BREAKING OPEN GOD'S STORY

The Word of God

Sometime before the meeting, the leader asks a member of the group to be prepared to proclaim the passage from the Gospel according to Luke.

Luke 24:13-35

The Road to Emmaus

Reader *The Gospel of the Lord.*

All **Praise to you, Lord Jesus Christ.**

Reflect

Moment of silent reflection

- What word, phrase, or image from the Scripture reading touches my heart or speaks to my life?

Invitation to Share

The leader invites those who so wish to echo a key word or phrase that touched them from the Scripture passage.

Reflection

What does it mean to follow in the footsteps of Christ? Behind the way the question is worded lies the metaphor of journey—a favorite metaphor that Luke uses both in his Gospel and in the Acts of the Apostles.

Of all the journeys Luke presents, perhaps the one we have just heard is the most appealing. It's very easy to identify ourselves with the two disciples, so troubled by the way things have turned out that they seem to think of themselves as ex-disciples. They literally turn their backs on Jerusalem.

They talk as they walk, but from the sadness on their faces, they just seem to be reinforcing each other's confusion.

Then a "stranger" joins them. In Luke's Gospel, the "stranger" and others on the margins of society have a special place in Jesus' compassion: we'll see a remarkable example of that in session five.

In the Emmaus story the stranger poses some straightforward questions, and persuades the two disciples to share their sadness. They talk of Jesus of Nazareth, how he proved himself a prophet by what he said and did. But that was while he was still with them. The problem is, he was sentenced to death and crucified. They have heard rumors from women (they seem to imply this is therefore unreliable) that he is alive, but all they know for certain is the tomb is empty. For them, Jesus' promises now seem to be equally empty.

The stranger reprimands them for not believing (he doesn't say "understanding," but "believing") the *full* message of the prophets. You can't pick and choose, he seems to say, the bits of Scripture you like! The Word of God can be consolation, but it is also a challenge. The Christ does bring good news, but the way to the fullness of that Good News is through his suffering and death.

How long did the conversation last? Not long enough for the two disciples who urge the stranger to stay. But long enough for the stranger to convert what they saw only as bad news to good news, to transform their grief and anguish into hope and joy. It is during their evening meal together that he breaks bread, and they recognize Jesus in the stranger.

At that moment Jesus disappears. But this is no longer a cause of anxiety for the disciples. Exactly the opposite. They now speak of "our hearts burning within us." They set out immediately and return to Jerusalem where they discover their good news matches the Good News. Luke doesn't say it explicitly, but don't you get the impression that though the disciples were walking toward Emmaus, they rush back to Jerusalem? Their lives now have meaning, purpose!

What can we learn from these two disciples who were among the first to faith share after and about the Resurrection? Perhaps that being a follower of Christ is less about us walking with Christ and more about letting him walk with us. Perhaps not to let anxiety blind us to the presence of Christ in the stranger. Certainly to be attentive to the fullness of God's message to us in Scripture, and open to reading our lives through the eyes of faith as the fulfillment of that Word. Certainly that while grief and anguish may be part of our lives, and the lives of others, we are called to convert these into hope and joy. The turning point in the story is the breaking of bread: so, too, for us, the Eucharist should be the "source and summit." Their Eucharistic experience "immediately" pushes them to get back on the road—this time in the right direction!

Following in Christ's footsteps means heading for Jerusalem, where

Where is Emmaus?

Emmaus "... has not been definitively identified, ... in fact it represents all places. The road leading there is the road each Christian, indeed all mankind, follows. The risen Jesus becomes our traveling companion on the roads of our life, to rekindle in our hearts the flame of faith and hope and to break the bread of eternal life.

The drama faced by the disciples of Emmaus appears to mirror the situation of many Christians of our own time. It seems as if the hope of faith has failed. Faith itself is in crisis because of negative experiences that make us feel we have been abandoned by the Lord. But this road to Emmaus along which we are walking can become a path of purification and maturity for our belief in God."

Benedict XVI,
Midday Message, April 6, 2008

Christ's mission reaches fulfillment. Baptism makes Christ's mission ours; in Baptism we promise to walk with Christ, and he promises to walk with us.

Intriguingly, there were *two* disciples on the road. We are baptized into the Church, a community. We'll reflect, with help from Saint Paul and Vatican II, on the meaning of being a community in session three.

For us, as for the two disciples, everything hinges on the Resurrection that we already share in Baptism. In that sacrament, and in every Sunday Eucharist, we proclaim with confidence and faith, as did the two disciples, "He is risen!" This is a proclamation we are called to make, not just in words, but in action. Our lives are to be a constant invitation to others to ***"ARISE Together in Christ!"***

Invitation to Share

Take a few moments of silence to reflect on the following questions. Then share your reflections.

1. To which part of the Emmaus story do I most relate? Is there anything in the story that surprises me?
2. The two disciples on the road to Emmaus do not recognize Jesus until he is gone. Recount a time when you only recognized the presence of Christ in hindsight.
3. Share an experience of your "heart burning within you" either from personal reading of Scripture, or from faith sharing on Scripture in your ***ARISE*** group.
4. How can I make what is good news in my life into a message of Good News for others?

INVITATION TO ACT

Sharing and being together in a small Christian community fosters growth in our faith and in our spirituality. But no communal sharing is complete without a serious commitment to putting our faith into practice.

In this session we have reflected on what it means to walk in the footsteps of Christ: to what kind of action does this inspire us?

Some Suggestions

1. Take time to reread today's Scripture. Imagine yourself in the text, as the unnamed disciple. Then, in a spirit of prayer, reflect on the following questions: What is it that saddens me? What am I running away from? What would the stranger reprimand me for not believing? In what way will I turn around and get back on track for "Jerusalem"?
2. Christ is present in the "stranger." Commit to an action that "recognizes" the strangers in your community. For example, go out of your way to speak to someone you do not know at next Sunday's Mass.
3. Determine, either personally or with others from the group, concrete ways by which you can bring sad and disillusioned members of the community back to joy and hope.

Closing Prayer

All **Lord, make me know your ways,**
teach me your paths.
Guide me in your truth and teach me,
for you are God, my Savior.

(Psalm 25:4-5)

Reader 1 Jesus says:
"I am the Way and the Truth and the Life.
No one comes to the Father
except through me."

(John 14:6)

All **Lord, make me know your ways,**
teach me your paths.
Guide me in your truth and teach me,
for you are God, my Savior.

Reader 2 "Were not our hearts burning within us
while he was talking to us on the road,
while he was opening the Scriptures to us?"
(Luke 24:32)

All **Lord, make me know your ways,**
teach me your paths.
Guide me in your truth and teach me,
for you are God, my Savior.

Suggested Song
We Walk by Faith

Looking Ahead

Prepare for the next faith-sharing meeting by reading over Session Two.

In particular:

- *read the **"Focus for this Session"** (on page 21).*
- *Read the Gospel passage:* **Luke 4:14-22**. *It would help your appreciation of this episode if you read all the way through verse 30.*
- *Read the "Key Themes of Catholic Social Teaching," on pages 77-79.* There is a brief (nine minutes) but compelling presentation of these key themes in Part One of the DVD *In the Footsteps of Christ* (USCCB Publication No 5-444; available online at www.usccbpublishing.org).

Called to Christ's Mission Today

> *Believe what you read.*
> *Preach what you believe.*
> *Practice what you preach."*
>
> *Rite of Ordination of Deacons*

> *If you enter into relationship with a lonely or suffering person you will discover something else: that it is you who are being healed … If you will let yourself be molded thus by the cry of the poor and accept their healing friendship, then they may guide your footsteps into community and lead you into a new vision of humanity … into the kingdom Jesus speaks of."*
>
> Jean Vanier, *Befriending the Stranger*

Focus for this Session

- Empowered by the Spirit
- Christ builds his mission on the Word of God
- This mission is to bring Good News by word and by action
- The same Spirit, the same mission is entrusted to the Church
- How are we to be instruments of Good News in our world today?

GATHER

Introductions

If there are new members to the group since the first session, take a few moments to welcome them, and invite them to introduce themselves.

Opening Prayer

Leader Let us spend a few moments,
becoming more aware of God's presence ...
... God's presence in us and in this community,
gathered in Jesus' name.

Pause for a few moments of quiet.

3

Suggested Song

God Has Chosen Me

or

You Are Mine *(ARISE Songs for Season One* CD, Track 5*)*

Then one of the members reads the following prayer:

Lord,
may the people you call to work in the world
be effective witnesses to the truth of the Gospel
and make your Church a living presence
in the midst of the world.
We ask this through Christ our Lord.

(Adapted from prayers for the laity, Roman Missal)

All **Amen.**

Living Our Faith

Share briefly your experience of putting into effect the action you chose after the last session.

BREAKING OPEN OUR STORY

Reflection

"I just don't see it."

"I don't believe that we are."

"We don't really believe that."

What was the doubt about? It was about the idea that Lawrence, Massachusetts, is the poorest city in the state and one of the poorest in the country.

Lawrence, a former industrial center situated on the Merrimack River, has a population of more than 76,000 people, according to the 2010 U.S. Census. The city has a history of heavy immigration dating from the early nineteenth century, and the population now is more than 73 percent Latino.

Some members of St. Patrick's parish in Lawrence were skeptical about the level of poverty and hunger in this population.

"We don't know anybody that's hungry," one parishioner said.

Father Paul O'Brien, the Harvard-educated pastor at St. Patrick's, thought otherwise, and many of his parishioners agreed, and they did something about it.

Father O'Brien and a corps of volunteers created an organization to raise funds to build a center where anyone in the city could go for meals.

The campaign raised $1.4 million, which was used to build the "Cor Unum"–"One Heart"–meal center across from St. Patrick's church.

The organization–labelsareforjars.com–raises much of that money by selling black t-shirts that have the organization's logo across the back and a commonly-used negative term across the front–terms such as "homeless," "addict," "minority," "slacker," and "troubled teen."

The shirts are sold rolled up in plastic jars, which buyers are encouraged to fill with money to donate back to the project.

The purpose of the design is to undermine the labels that often are used to dehumanize people. It's an issue directly related to the food project in Lawrence.

"I'm not going to be a part of saying that somebody who needs food is not going to get food because that person has problems," Father O'Brien said.

And, in fact, when the center was about to open, volunteers didn't wait to see who would come; they went into Lawrence and invited people–from families in the park to homeless people under a bridge–handing out pamphlets that said, "All Are Welcome."

The Cor Unum Meal Center now serves meals seven days a week. The center is large enough to accommodate hundreds of people at each meal in a restaurant-like atmosphere in which a volunteer wait staff serves meals to guests at their tables. The center, which receives assistance from a regional food bank and numerous local businesses, also houses St. Patrick's food pantry which distributes non-perishable groceries to needy individuals and families.

We often observe the world and feel saddened by what we see. Our natural emotions may move us further to empathize with people we see suffering. The people of Lawrence showed more than empathy. They let it lead them to compassion, but then further to express that compassion in a real and determined way. That is what "solidarity" means.

"Solidarity is not a feeling of vague compassion or shallow distress at the misfortunes of so many people, both near and far. On the contrary, it is a firm and

The witness of solidarity

"Above all the Gospel must be proclaimed by witness. Take a Christian or a handful of Christians who, in the midst of their own community, show their capacity for understanding and acceptance, their sharing of life and destiny with other people, their solidarity with the efforts of all for whatever is noble and good. Let us suppose that, in addition, they radiate in an altogether simple and unaffected way their faith in values that go beyond current values, and their hope in something that is not seen and that one would not dare to imagine. Through this wordless witness these Christians stir up irresistible questions in the hearts of those who see how they live: Why are they like this? Why do they live in this way? What or who is it that inspires them?"

Paul VI, *Evangelii Nuntiandi*, 21

persevering determination to commit oneself to the common good, that is to say, to the good of all and of each individual because we are all really responsible for all" (Pope John Paul II, *Sollicitudo rei socialis*, 38 [Encyclical on the social concern of the Church]).

The first level of solidarity is listening to each other's stories, opening our eyes and ears to what is real in others' lives. The story we have shared is a profound example of how an awareness of others' needs grew naturally to a more decisive concrete gesture of solidarity. Father O'Brien called attention to a want, a need: the people who listened to him heard that as a call from God and acted on it. This is the well-tried and proven threefold process: see, judge, act. Pope John XXIII included it in his encyclical *Mater et Magistra*, as a way of putting social principles into practice.

- "See" means reviewing the concrete situation.
- "Judge" means coming to a decision, informed by the first step, but always in light of the principles
- "Act" means deciding in the circumstances what can and should be done.

For those who cannot afford food, a place were they are welcomed and fed as guests is Good News.

(Source: RENEW International's Faith-Sharing Edition DVD of *Scenes from a Parish*, a documentary film by James Rutenbeck)

Invitation to Share

Take a few moments of silence to reflect on one of the following questions. Then share your reflections.

1. Share a story that, for you, is an example of "solidarity."
2. "A first level of solidarity is listening to one another's stories." Share how well you feel the group is doing this in these sessions; above all, share what we can do to improve our ability to listen to one another.

3. With whom do you feel "interconnected"? Share about this, thinking of our interconnectedness at personal, church, national, and international levels.

BREAKING OPEN GOD'S STORY

The Word of God

Sometime before the meeting, the leader asks a member of the group to be prepared to proclaim the passage from the Gospel according to Luke.

Luke 4:14-22

The "Good News"

Reader *The Gospel of the Lord.*

All **Praise to you, Lord Jesus Christ.**

Reflect

Moment of silent reflection

- What word, phrase, or image from the Scripture reading touches my heart or speaks to my life?

Invitation to Share

The leader invites those who so wish to echo a key word or phrase that touched them from the Scripture passage.

Reflection

Can you remember your first day at work? The dreams and hopes that it represented ... and the reality of how the day actually turned out. There's a sense in which in today's Scripture Luke is sharing with us Jesus' first day at work. And it certainly is full of both great dreams and harsh reality.

Jesus proclaims his mission, clearly, unambiguously. It is to be the bearer of God's Good News. We'll explore the content of that mission in a moment, but first we should take time to see on what this great mission is founded.

The first foundation is the Holy Spirit (a key theme in the Gospel according to Luke). Luke clearly announces that Jesus is "filled with the Holy Spirit." Very significantly, Jesus' own opening words are "The spirit of the Lord is upon me ..."

The second foundation is the Word of God. Jesus places his mission clearly under the plan of salvation in Scripture set out by the prophet Isaiah, God's vision for his people. The reading is the promise of a new era of freedom and God's favor. It is a promise that those in the synagogue knew well, but on this day it takes on a freshness, a reality, because Jesus announces that what is promised is fulfilled, here and now, today. It is a message of hope that clearly struck a chord for the listeners, who are full of compliments for Jesus.

Jesus presents the key characteristics of his mission, his life's work, in the words of Isaiah (Isaiah 61:1-2):

— to bring good news to the poor
— to proclaim release to captives
— to proclaim recovery of sight to the blind
— to let the oppressed go free
— to proclaim the year of the Lord's favor.

An accumulation of magnificent metaphors that together suggest a fullness of salvation and liberation from all that oppresses us.

What might be our first response to this message? Like the people who heard Jesus in the synagogue, it should be appreciation. Let us thank God that we are the recipients of this liberation and salvation, fulfilled for us in Christ! The poverty of our human condition has been irrevocably enriched by Christ sharing our humanity. Our vision of humanity has been illuminated by Christ. The oppression of sin and the captivity of death which is part of our humanity has been vanquished by Christ's death and resurrection, in which we already share through Baptism.

But are we not being called to something deeper, inseparable from the first? The richness and the illumination we have received are not ours to be guarded jealously, but to be shared. Yes, we are called to ***ARISE***, but it is "***together***" and it is "***in Christ.***" Remember the one-line homily Jesus gives on the reading: God's promise, made through Isaiah, is fulfilled "today." That fulfillment here and now, today, is entrusted to us. This is why the U. S. Bishops say unequivocally "the social teaching of the Church is an essential part of Catholic faith" (see sidebar).

An essential part of Catholic faith

"Many Catholics do not adequately understand that the social teaching of the Church is an essential part of Catholic faith. This poses a serious challenge for all Catholics, since it weakens our capacity to be a Church that is true to the demands of the Gospel. We need to do more to share the social mission and message of our Church."

USCCB, *Sharing Catholic Social Teaching: Challenges and Directions*

As Luke's Gospel unfolds, we see Jesus as the living expression of God's solidarity, reaching out in compassion to those who were on the margins of society: to lepers, to women, to foreigners. Luke shows us a Jesus who worked out the implications of his mission in his every "today."

What are the implications of that same mission for our "today"? Where are the blind-spots in our society and culture, and how can we shed light on them? What are the worst forms of poverty rampant in our modern world, and what is the Good News we have to bring? What are the forms of oppression, subtle or blatant, in our community and society structures? How are we, and/or others, enslaved by them? How are we to offer freedom from these?

Challenging questions—we may feel so daunted by the challenge that we avoid them. Daunting indeed if we begin with the questions. But that is not where today's Scripture begins. "Filled with the Holy Spirit ..."; "The spirit of the Lord is upon me ..." This, as it was for Christ, is the firm foundation on which we stand. The same Spirit that empowered and enabled Jesus in his mission is given to us, empowering and enabling us.

Where are we to turn to begin shaping our answers? We have the unambiguous example given by Jesus himself: we look to the Word of God, to the vision of humanity and of creation that is entrusted to us by the biblical stories, poems, prophecies, songs, letters, and Gospels. Scripture sets out God's dream-for us. The social teaching of the Church points to the principles and values that lie at the heart of this dream. But the bottom line, converting these dreams, principles, and values into reality, is up to us.

When we express solidarity, and we start to show a firm determination to work for the common good, we may be dismissively accused by some of having "an agenda." Indeed we do—but it is not *our* agenda. It's an agenda set by God and modeled by Christ. The "good news" is not something merely read from a sacred text (though that is an important starting point); it is a sacred "to do" list. What Christ promises in words, he fulfills in action. Christ did not *write* a Gospel; he *lived* one.

Jesus clearly believed what he read;
he preached what he believed;
he practiced what he preached.

Invitation to Share

Take a few moments of silence to reflect on the following questions. Then share your reflections.

1. What are the blindnesses from which our society and culture suffer today? What holds us and those around us captive in our lives today? What will be our first steps in seeking to bring light and freedom to these situations?
2. Think of someone whom you would describe as "empowered and enabled by the Spirit." Share what it is about their life and their actions that leads you to say this.
3. In our opening prayer we asked God to help us give "effective witness to the Gospel." What does this mean today for me, for our faith-sharing group, for our parish, for our diocese?

INVITATION TO ACT

Sharing and being together in a small Christian community fosters growth in our faith and in our spirituality. But no communal sharing is complete without a serious commitment to putting our faith into practice.

In this session we have reflected on Christ's mission and our call to continue that mission in today's society: to what kind of action does this inspire us?

Some Suggestions

1. What will I do this week that will be "good news" for someone? Re-read today's Gospel passage. Identify a simple act of solidarity (based on today's Gospel) and commit to put it into action this coming week.
2. What will I/we do in the coming week to make the Church's social teaching more readily available to members of our parish? Contact your diocesan social action office, and/or visit one these USCCB websites:
   - Justice, Peace and Human Development www.usccb.org/sdwp
   - Catholic Campaign for Human Development www.usccb.org/cchd
   - Catholic Relief Services www.crs.org
   - Catholic Charities www.catholiccharitiesusa.org
3. The story of Cor Unum, a center that has dramatically reduced hunger among the people of Lawrence, Mass., is told in James Rutenbeck's documentary film *Scenes from a Parish*. Through the experiences of parishioners of St. Patrick's Church in Lawrence, the film examines the challenge of the commandment to love your neighbor when the ethnicity and the social and economic standing of your neighbors are changing–and your city and parish are changing as a result. Introduce your parish to RENEW

International's edition DVD of *Scenes from a Parish*, which is accompanied by faith-sharing resource.

Closing Prayer

Leader Confident that Christ has entrusted his Spirit to us,
we make our own the promises we are called to fulfill:

Members of the group take it in turn to read aloud the promise from Isaiah as follows:

Reader 1 The Spirit of the Lord is upon me,
because he has anointed me
to bring good news to the poor.

Pause

Reader 2 The Spirit of the Lord is upon me,
because he has anointed me
and sent me to proclaim release to the captives.

Pause

Reader 3 The Spirit of the Lord is upon me,
because he has anointed me
and sent me to proclaim recovery of sight
to the blind.

Pause

Reader 4 The Spirit of the Lord is upon me,
because he has anointed me
and sent me to let the oppressed go free.

Pause

Reader 5 The Spirit of the Lord is upon me,
because he has anointed me
and sent me to proclaim
the year of the Lord's favor.

Pause

Leader We have already been baptized into Christ
and in Confirmation we have already been sealed
with the power of his Spirit.
Our way of life should at all times
reflect the goodness of Christ.
With God's help,
may we be active members of the Church,

alive in Jesus Christ.
Under the guidance of the Holy Spirit
may we give our lives completely
in the service of all,
following in the footsteps of Christ.
Let us pray together.

All **May God our Father complete**
the work we have begun
and keep the gifts of the Holy Spirit
active in our hearts.
Make us ready to live the Gospel
and eager to do God's will.
May we never be ashamed
to proclaim to all the world Christ crucified
living and reigning for ever and ever.
Amen.

(Based on the Instruction and the Prayer over the People from the Rite of Confirmation*)*

Suggested Song

Take the Word of God with You

or

We Are Called *(ARISE Songs for Season One* CD, Track 17*)*

Looking Ahead

Prepare for the next faith-sharing meeting by reading over Session Three.

In particular:

- *read the **"Focus for this Session"** (on page 33).*
- *Read the Scripture passage: **1 Corinthians 12:12-14, 24-27**. It would help you set this passage in context if you were to read all of chapters 12 and 13.*
- *Reread the "Key Themes of Catholic Social Teaching," on pages 77-79.* There is a brief (nine minutes) but compelling presentation of these key themes in Part One of the DVD *In the Footsteps of Christ* (USCCB Publication No 5-444; available online at www.usccbpublishing.org).

SESSION 3

Called to Bring Joy and Hope

> *"The Church is the Body of Christ… Christ, who once was dead and is now risen, establishes the community of believers as his own Body… In the unity of this Body, there is a diversity of members and functions. All members are linked to one another, especially to those who are suffering, to the poor and persecuted."*
>
> *Catechism of the Catholic Church*, 805-806

> *"A Eucharist which does not pass over into the concrete practice of love is intrinsically fragmented."*
>
> Benedict XVI, *Deus Caritas Est*, 14

Focus for this Session

- The social teaching of the Church is an essential part of Catholic faith
- This is founded on believing:
  - — we are members of the Body of Christ
  - — there is an essential bond that unites the community that is the Church with the community that is humanity
  - — we are called to bring joy and hope to all
- We are called to discern what is "truly human": to reject the culture of death and promote the culture of life

GATHER

Opening Prayer

Leader All-powerful and ever-living God,
may our joys and hopes match the dream
you have for each of us
and for all humanity.
Be with us in our griefs and anxieties,
to turn our weakness into strength.
In both our joys and our sorrows
give us the courage to live in faithful witness to you.
We ask this through Christ your Son,
who walked the way of humanity,
that we may walk in his footsteps.

All **Amen.**

Suggested Song

One Bread, One Body

or

All Are Welcome

(ARISE Songs for Season One CD, Track 10*)*

Living Our Faith

Share briefly your experience of putting into effect the action you chose after the last session.

BREAKING OPEN OUR STORY

Reflection

In Brooklyn, in August 1980 Jennifer Sullivan celebrated her 16th birthday. Her aunt, Sister Ita Ford, a Maryknoll missioner in El Salvador, wrote to her hoping it would be "a special day." Her letter says:

"I want to say something to you and I wish I were there to talk to you because sometimes letters don't get across all the meaning and feeling. But I'll give it a try anyway.

What I want to say—some of it isn't too jolly birthday talk, but it's real.

Yesterday I stood looking down at a 16-year-old who had been killed a few hours earlier. I know a lot of kids even younger who are dead.

This is a terrible time in El Salvador. A lot of idealism and commitment is getting snuffed out here now. The reasons why so many people are being killed are quite complicated, yet there are some clear, simple strands.

One is that many people have found a meaning to their life, to sacrifice, struggle, and even to death. And whether their life span is 16 years, 60 or 90, for them, their life has had a purpose. In many ways they are fortunate people,

Brooklyn is not passing through the drama of El Salvador, but some things hold true wherever one is, at whatever age.

What I'm saying is, I hope you come to find that which gives life a deep meaning for you—something worth living for, maybe even worth dying for—something that energizes you, enthuses you, enables you to keep moving ahead. I can't tell you what it might be—that's for you to find, to love. I can just encourage you to start looking, and support you in the search.

I hope this doesn't sound like some kind of sermon because I don't mean it that way. Rather, it's something you learn here, and I want to share it with you. In fact, it's my birthday present to you. If it doesn't make sense right at this moment, keep this and read it sometime from now. Maybe it will be clearer. Or ask me about it, OK?"

There would be no Christmas letter from aunt to niece. In December of that same year, Sister Ita Ford was raped and murdered along with three other American churchwomen (Jean Donovan, Sister Dorothy Kazel, and Sister Maura Clarke). Their day-in, day-out life was one of service to the people of El Salvador: delivering food and supplies to needy families, transporting refugees, accompanying grief-stricken families whose relatives had "disappeared."

They themselves became victims of the relentless campaign of violence they were there to fight, not with violence but with love. Sister Ita had written to her sister:

"If you choose to enter into other people's suffering, to love others, you at least have to consent in some way to the possible consequences. Actually what I have learned here is that death is not the worst evil. We look death in the face every day. But the cause of the death is evil. That's what we have to wrestle and fight against."

Sister Maura Clarke wrote, only weeks before her death, "If we leave the people when they suffer the cross, how credible is our word to them? The Church's role is to accompany those who suffer the most, and to witness our hope in the resurrection."

To witness our hope in the resurrection ... to proclaim ***"ARISE!"*** not just by our words but above all in what we do.

Invitation to Share

Take a few moments of silence to reflect on one of the following questions. Then share your reflections.

1. What sparks of hope do I see in the words of Sister Ita Ford? What is the deepest grief and anxiety she expresses? Are these her own hopes and anxieties, or those of others?
2. If you were writing to a 16 year-old in your family, what are the deep hopes and anxieties you would mention?
3. What is it that Sister Ita and Sister Maura both name as the source of the meaning in what they are doing?

BREAKING OPEN GOD'S STORY

The Word of God

Some time before the meeting, the leader asks a member of the group to be prepared to proclaim the passage from St. Paul's First Letter to the Corinthians.

1 Corinthians 12:12-14, 24-27

One body in Christ

Reader *The Word of the Lord.*

All **Thanks be to God.**

Reflect

Moment of silent reflection

- What word, phrase, or image from the Scripture reading touches my heart or speaks to my life?

Invitation to Share

The leader invites those who so wish to echo a key word or phrase that touched them from the Scripture passage.

Reflection

Just over a decade after Jesus' death and resurrection, the Church faced a major decision: should the Church remain solely within its Jewish roots; or should it reach out and welcome Gentiles to the Christian faith, as Gentiles, without expecting them first to become Jews. The crucial underlying question was whether the Good News of Christ was culture-bound (in this case, with Judaism), or whether the task of the Church was to evangelize whatever culture people belonged to (in this case, Gentiles). The question was debated by the apostles and elders at what we consider the Church's first ever Council at Jerusalem, around AD 48 (recorded in Acts 15). The decision: the Good News is to be proclaimed to all peoples, as they are. They should not be asked to abandon their culture, but only to liberate themselves from those things within their culture that are foreign to the Gospel.

We remember Paul as Apostle to the Gentiles, whose apostolate was true to both parts of the Council's decision: he reached out to the pagans; but he consistently made it clear what parts of their culture they should leave behind.

Paul's theology and the vision of the Church that he preached was founded on the central belief that through baptism we are incorporated into Christ. We are connected not just to Christ, but to everyone else who is connected to Christ. Put simply, we are members of the Body of Christ. Paul invites us to use what we know about the human body and its members to help us understand what it means to be a member of the Body of Christ. Each member of our human body has a different role, but they have to work in harmony: many parts; one single body. What has to unite us is not our culture (Paul refers explicitly to the major cultural differences of his time: the members can be Jews or Gentiles, slaves or free). What unites us is the one Spirit in which we are baptized. "There is one Body, one Spirit ... One Lord, one faith, one Baptism" (Ephesians 4:4-5). This unity

"No man is an island"

"The church is catholic, universal, so are all her actions; all that she does belongs to all. When she baptizes a child, that action concerns me; for that child is thereby connected to that head which is my head too, and ingrafted into the body whereof I am a member. And when she buries a man, that action concerns me: all mankind is of one author and is one volume; when one man dies, one chapter is not torn out of the book, but translated into a better language; and every chapter must be so translated. God employs several translators; some pieces are translated by age, some by sickness, some by war, some by justice; but God's hand is in every translation, and his hand shall bind up all our scattered leaves again for that library where every book shall lie open to one another....

No man is an island, entire of itself; every man is a piece of the continent, a part of the main. If a clod be washed away by the sea, Europe is the less, as well as if promontory were, as well as if a manor of thy friend's or of thine own were. Any man's death diminishes me, because I am involved in mankind; and therefore never send to know for whom the bell tolls; it tolls for thee."

John Donne (1572-1631)
from Meditation XVII

is so total, Paul says, that whatever affects one member affects the whole body: "If one member suffers, all suffer together with it; if one member is honored, all rejoice together with it" (1 Corinthians 12:26).

Some 1900 years or so after that first Council in Jerusalem, the Church again gathered for what we call the Second Vatican Council (1962-65). The concern was the same: how the Church should be reaching out to the world of our time. The Council's answers were expressed in many documents (on the liturgy, on the Church, on the Word of God, on relations with other Christians, and other faiths, etc.). But in a special way this question is answered by the Council's final document, the *Pastoral Constitution on the Church in the Modern World*. It begins:

"The joys and the hopes, the griefs and the anxieties of the men of this age, especially those who are poor or in any way afflicted, these are the joys and hopes, the griefs and anxieties of the followers of Christ. Indeed, nothing genuinely human fails to raise an echo in their hearts" (*Gaudium et Spes*, 1).

The challenge for us, as members of the Body of Christ in the world of today is to discern and work for what is "genuinely human." Our vision of the dignity of the human person is founded on believing that each human person is created in the image and likeness of God; that God in Christ shares our humanity; that Christ brings redemption to all, and through him we are adopted daughters and sons; that we are called to community with God for all eternity. Vatican II teaches us that there is nothing in being Christian that separates us from others, but rather gives us greater reason, in faith, for our fundamental unity. The hope-filled vision of Vatican II is founded on what it describes as "a new humanism," in which the human person is defined by "responsibility to his brothers and sisters and toward history" (*Gaudium et Spes*, 55).

The message of Paul to the community of the early Church at Corinth has lost none of its relevance: we are called to be Church in, to, and for the world; to the culture, and the society in which we find ourselves.

This does not mean we have to reject everything about our modern culture. It does mean that we have to look at it critically, and unmask the reality of the way we live, and, in particular, how the way we live has consequences for others.

We can be rightly proud of what Pope John Paul II called the American experiment: "an experiment in which men and women would enjoy equality of rights and opportunities in the pursuit of happiness and in service to the common good." But we need to ask, what has happened to the vision of "freedom" on which our culture is built? Has it become freedom, even unfettered license, for some at the expense of others? The original vision enshrined freedom as a way that not only allowed but enabled people to fulfill their duties and responsibilities toward the family and toward the common good.

The Culture of Death

"Whatever is opposed to life itself, such as any type of murder, genocide, abortion, euthanasia or willful self-destruction, whatever violates the integrity of the human person, such as mutilation, torments inflicted on body or mind, attempts to coerce the will itself; whatever insults human dignity, such as subhuman living conditions, arbitrary imprisonment, deportation, slavery, prostitution, the selling of women and children; as well as disgraceful working conditions, where men are treated as mere tools for profit, rather than as free and responsible persons; all these things and others of their like are infamies indeed. They poison human society, but they do more harm to those who practice them than those who suffer from the injury. Moreover, they are supreme dishonor to the Creator."

Gaudium et Spes, 27

This discernment is more difficult than we might imagine, simply because we ourselves belong to this culture, so there are certain attitudes and values that have become second nature to us. To question our culture is in a very real sense to question ourselves. We need to sustain the change of heart we explored throughout Season Two.

The Church, echoing Scripture, reminds us we are called to discern what in our culture will support the joys and hopes of people, and use that deliberately and fully to bring them the Good News of full and genuine humanity in Christ; to discern, too, what in our culture is the cause of people's griefs and anxieties, and to reject these by refusing to be part of them, by denouncing them for what they are, and working to eradicate them (see sidebar on page 40). John Paul II spoke of how our society is "marked by a dramatic struggle between the 'culture of life' and the 'culture of death'" (*Evangelium Vitae*, 95).

The Christian response, though, is not just to list what constitutes the "culture of death." We are called to promote the victory of life over death that lies at the heart of our faith, so "we need to develop a deeply critical sense capable of discerning true values and authentic needs." (Pope John-Paul II, *Evangelium Vitae* 95).

Our mission as Church is to discern and work for what is "genuinely human." This is the purpose of our faith, this is why we are called to charity, this is the hope entrusted to us that we have to share with the world. We are called to nothing less than to shape history in terms of the Good News proclaimed and embodied by Jesus. That is our joy and our hope.

True values and authentic needs (An overview of Gaudium et Spes)

Gaudium et Spes, in Part One, sets out truly human values:

- The inherent dignity of the human person
- The essentially social nature of the human person

This leads, in Part Two, to outlining five areas of urgent concern:

- the dignity of marriage and the family
- the proper development of culture
- socio-economic life
- the life of the political community and
- the promotion of peace and the community of peoples.

Invitation to Share

Take a few moments of silence to reflect on the following questions. Then share your reflections.

1. Pope John Paul II spoke of the "need to develop a deep critical sense capable of discerning true values and authentic needs":
   — from your sharing, compile a list of what you believe should count as "true values."
   — from your sharing, compile a list of what you believe should count as "authentic needs."

In what way can I, or we as a group, promote these values and/or respond to one of these needs?

2. Share your experiences of how being a member of a small community has helped you relate better to the Church as a community, and helped your engagement to the larger community. Be open to sharing in ways that prompt you toward action that will improve community life.
3. Compile a list, either personally or as group, of things that constitute the culture of death or a threat to a culture of life. Use this list in helping to decide your action steps throughout and beyond this Season of ***ARISE***.

INVITATION TO ACT

Sharing and being together in a small Christian community fosters growth in our faith and in our spirituality. But no communal sharing is complete without a serious commitment to putting our faith into practice.

In this session we have reflected on our call to bring "joy and hope," to discern and work for what is "truly human." To what kind of action does this inspire us?

Some Suggestions

1. Read *Gaudium et Spes.* (The complete text can be found online at the Vatican website www.vatican.va). What are some of the hopes that have been fulfilled? How many of the things it called "urgent" when it was published in 1965 still challenge us today? Are there other "anxieties and griefs" that you would add? Share these with your small community at the next session.
2. Perhaps you could arrange and prepare a Mass for the parish, to be celebrated at the conclusion of this Season. This would be in thanksgiving to God for the joys and hopes fulfilled; but at the same time, praying for the strength of God's Spirit to

read the signs of the times and work in the areas of ongoing challenge. Consider using the *Eucharistic Prayer for Masses for Various Needs and Occasions III*, on the theme "Jesus, Our Way to the Father."

3. Build on your sharing on the "culture of life/ culture of death" list. What will I do this week to promote life? What will I do to limit the influence of the culture of death? For example, identify a concern at either local or national level, and write to your local or national representative and/or to the papers about it.

The Common Good

"The catholicity of the Church is manifested in the active joint responsibility and generous cooperation of all for the sake of the common good."

John-Paul II, *Slavorum Apostoli*
(Encyclical on Saints Cyril and Methodius)

Closing Prayer

Leader Father,
you have given all peoples one common origin,
and your will is to gather them
as one family in yourself.
Fill the hearts of all with the fire of your love
and the desire to ensure justice
for all our sisters and brothers.
By sharing the good things you give us
may we secure justice and equality
for every human being,
an end to division,
and a human society built on love and peace.
We ask this through Christ our Lord.

All **Amen.**

Suggested Songs

6

We Are Many Parts

or

The Summons *(ARISE Songs for Season One* CD, Track 12*)*

Looking Ahead

Prepare for the next faith-sharing meeting by reading over Session Four.

In particular:

- *read the **"Focus for this Session"*** *(on page 45).*
- *Read the Scripture passage: **Genesis 18:1-10**. It would help you set this passage in context if you were to read Genesis 18:1-15, and Genesis 21:1-7.*
- *Reread the "Key Themes of Catholic Social Teaching," on pages 77-79.* There is a brief (nine minutes) but compelling presentation of these key themes in Part One of the DVD *In the Footsteps of Christ* (USCCB Publication No 5-444; available online at www.usccbpublishing.org).

Called to Lifegiving Love

SESSION 4

"They do not love who do not show their love."

William Shakespeare

*"Love is our origin,
love is our constant calling,
love is our fulfillment in heaven."*

Preface for Marriage III, *Roman Missal*

*"Each of us is the result of a thought of God.
Each of us is willed, each of us is loved, each of us is necessary."*

Benedict XVI, Homily, April 24, 2005

"Being family is a matter of hearts stretched and torn to love beyond our own selves. To welcome and then to let go of each other is to love like God and allow oneself to be loved by God."

Wendy M. Wright

Focus for this Session

- We are designed and destined by God for love
- Marriage as a "sacrament," a window into God, above all God as love.
- Challenges facing married couples and families today:
  — living faithfully
  — giving life
  — growing in mutuality
  — taking time
- The family as Church; the Church as family

GATHER

Opening Prayer

All Pray Together

We bless your name, O Lord,
for sending your own incarnate Son,
to live as part of a family,
so that, as he lived its life,
he would experience its worries and joys.
We ask you, Lord,
to protect and watch over our families,
so that in the strength of your grace
its members may enjoy prosperity,
possess the priceless gift of your peace,
and, as the Church alive in the home,
bear witness in this world to your glory.
We ask this through Christ our Lord. Amen.

Adapted from *Catholic Household Blessings and Prayers*
USCCB Committee on the Liturgy (Revised edition 2007)

Suggested Song

When Love Is Found

or

Gather Us In *(ARISE Songs for Season One* CD, Track 1*)*

Living Our Faith

Share briefly your experience of putting into effect the action you chose after the last session.

BREAKING OPEN OUR STORY

Reflection

Mike and Rosemary, very good friends of ours in South-East England, decided to celebrate their 25th wedding anniversary in a major way. It was modeled on a wedding reception: a very tasty meal, and speeches ... except that at the time of their wedding it was not part of the tradition for the bride to give a speech. This, they decided, was an opportunity to balance that.

Mike is very fulfilled person. He has a good job that comfortably supports his family. He is a gifted musician, very much at home on keyboard or guitar. He is active in several sports, notably skiing, and successfully completed the London marathon a couple of times. He is generous, outgoing. And Mike is blind—as a baby sitting in his carriage in the garden during World War II, his sight was destroyed by the pressure blast from a bomb that fell nearby.

It's true of all families, but somehow Mike's disability more clearly highlights how each of us depends on others for our own qualities to flourish. His parents, who made the heart-wrenching decision to send him as soon as possible to a boarding school for the blind. They "lost" a blind child, and gained a fulfilled son. His wife Rosemary, who is quite simply at his side when she knows he needs that; but who knows when to leave him so that, even as an adult, he learns by experience to improve his independence.

The bomb-blast happened when Mike was so young that he does not remember being able to see. All of us who know Mike, his beautiful wife Rosemary, and his good-looking children have been struck by the painful irony that he would never see any of this beauty. If you asked Mike about this he could give pithy, deep one-line answers. However, the bigger, fuller answer was given by Mike and Rosemary's fundamental attitude: "This is who I am; this is the person I love; this is who we are." Life for them was not "a problem," but an opportunity, an opportunity that they seized, very often with wit and humor.

There was, then, a delicious poignancy to how Rosemary ended her 25th wedding anniversary speech. She thought back to before they were married, before they had even met. She reminisced aloud how she had asked God: "Lord, please help me find a good husband. Please make him tall, dark, and handsome ..." She paused, and then switched to talking to God today: "But you know, Lord, when I said I didn't mind about his eyes, I meant the color!"

Invitation to Share

Take a few moments of silence to reflect on one of the following questions. Then share your reflections.

1. Recall a poignant moment from your family history, and share why it touches you.
2. Loving means holding on when it is needed, and letting go when it is needed. Share moments of your own experiences of "holding on" and "letting go."

BREAKING OPEN GOD'S STORY

The Word of God

Sometime before the meeting, the leader asks a member of the group to be prepared to proclaim the passage from the Book of Genesis.

Genesis 18:1-10

Abraham, Sarah, and the visitors

Reader *The Word of the Lord.*

All **Thanks be to God.**

Reflect

Moment of silent reflection

- What word, phrase, or image from the Scripture reading touched my heart or spoke to my life?

Invitation to Share

The leader invites those who so wish to echo a key word or phrase that touched them from the Scripture passage.

Reflection

This reflection will focus on the family and on marriage. That does not mean that the exchange is limited to those who experience marriage as spouses. After all, at a wedding in Cana it was a single guest who played a significant role in the success of the celebration! Whatever our life experience—whether we are single, separated, or divorced; with or without children—let us be open to seeing in what way through reflection and commitment to action, we can turn the water in our relationships into wine.

If we each had to write down stories about our family, what a variety of emotions and events they would include: poignant moments; moments of sadness, disappointment, disaster even; but, of course, moments of pleasure, joy, and fulfillment.

What these stories have in common is they are about sharing, and they all concern "love" (the moments of greatest sadness are probably those when that love faded, so still a reflection of that love).

There is no higher way to speak of marriage than to call it a "sacrament." Marriage speaks to us of God, of the nature of God, and above all, of God as love. Marriage speaks of God first and foremost to the couple and to their children; but thereafter, as they live the interrelationship of love, it speaks of God to others who see this.

The U.S. Bishops, in their document *Follow the Way of Love,* invite us to explore four qualities that lie at the heart of family life. Sadly, these are qualities or values that are the antithesis of our fast, short-term, competitive, and self-gratifying modern culture. That is why the Bishops call them "challenges." They are:

— living faithfully

— giving life

— growing in mutuality

— taking time

These four qualities can also be considered as opportunities. Opportunities that can help us as we work out the practicalities of marriage, and more generally, of family life today. But through and beyond that they can help us explore marriage as "sacrament," a window into God. In other words, do the four ways of behaving not reflect exactly how God acts with us?

Living faithfully

We often lament how difficult marriage is in today's culture. It's true. But we are not the first generation to face this; the centuries-old traditional words pledge being true in "good times and in bad." Marriage is a promise built on a mutual decision to love one another, come what may. That is not a one-time decision, but has to be reaffirmed, day in, day out.

There are plenty of solid, simply human reasons for insisting that the relationship be lasting and stable, not least for the sake of children. In seeing marriage as "sacrament" we are proclaiming something more: it is by seeing fidelity lived out in human relationships of love that we get a glimpse of God's unconditional love for us. The first witnesses to this are the couple themselves. God has given me my spouse so that through him/her, I come closer God.

In life, all the commitments we make—to the extent that they are founded on love and are faithfully carried through—are witness to God's faithfulness and love.

Giving Life

The vows that are exchanged before the community at a marriage are pregnant with promise. The couple promise not just who they are now, but who they can become together. It is a pledge of love that is the source of new life.

The first meaning of giving life is obviously the physical one, and this already implies an openness to welcoming children. Through the eyes of faith we see this as God choosing to include us as partners in the ongoing "work" of creation. Just as one of the creation narratives portrays God breathing his Spirit into the person modeled from the dust of the soil, so, too, the couple are called to give a dimension of life that is spiritual. This implies nurturing and education not just in the practicalities of life, but passing on values, principles, and assuring that the God-given gift of faith has what it needs to grow.

This larger sense of giving life includes the way we welcome people into our family; this could be in the very special sense of adopting a child. It can also be the way we reach out to assist and support other families. Whenever we help in educating others, we are giving life to their minds; this includes passing on not only our own wisdom but also the faith of the Church, and the vision of true human values and a culture of life that we explored in session three.

Giving life is about the way we contribute to the community: to the world, and to the Church. How will the world be a better place thanks to what we pass on to the next generation? How will the Church be a more vibrant sign of Christ's presence in the world thanks to our children?

The family as "domestic Church"

"Many profound bonds link the Church and the Christian family and establishing the family as a 'Church in miniature' (*ecclesia domestica*), in such a way that the family is a living image and historical representation of the Church."

John Paul II, *Familiaris Consortio*, 49

Growing in mutuality

Marriage is fundamentally a partnership. Our faith tradition tells us it is together that man and woman are the image and likeness of God. We are one in our being children of God; we are made even more one in Christ (see Galatians 3:27-28). Yet in marriage we come together as man and woman precisely because we are different, and in need of the other.

Mutuality can and will mean that the husband and wife play different roles, but it is not just about sharing tasks, deciding who does what. Mutuality is about having a common dream, and then working together to make that dream a reality. In marriage, the dream is about the fulfillment of each person and of the couple as a couple.

As family, and as Church, we rejoice in whatever different God-given qualities we each have, and we give them space to become the source of mutual enrichment in a spirit of partnership, and in, a very real sense, of "communion."

This sense of mutuality will be all the richer the more we involve our extended family. Elders can have an especially enriching influence, because they are "a witness to the past and a source of wisdom for the young and for the future" *(Familiaris Consortio,* 27)

Mutuality is essential for the couple. Mutuality is also the basis for the fundamental attitude of respect for the other that should color all our relationships, i.e., what does it mean to be someone's child? What does it mean to be someone's sister/brother? What does it mean to be grandparent/grandchild? It is an attitude that will keep all our friendships healthy and generous. A lived-out mutuality will also help us to a richer appreciation of what it means to be "Church": our Baptism implies a sharing in the mutual ministry of love (see *Anointing of the Sick,* 33).

Taking time

Time is a God-given part of creation; on the seventh day God makes rest. It is a gift that as a couple, and that as families we need to share with each other. Time is what gives love the space for intimacy, understanding, and what ultimately enables love to grow.

The busyness of our modern society can eat into our loving relationships. Long working hours, plus the logistics of getting each member of the family where they need to be for school, sports, medical appointments, shopping, even community and church volunteering—all very valid and necessary activities—can fragment our family life. We need to choose to spend time together as families, so that they become places of genuine sharing: of our joys and hopes; but also our griefs and anxieties.

If, through the eyes of faith, we see time as a God-given gift, should we not in return be giving time to God? Of course, this should be part of the life of anyone who claims to be walking in the footsteps of Christ: but in the light of our reflection today, we also need to consider how we give time together, as a family, to God—not least by sharing as a family in the life of the bigger family of Church at the Sunday Eucharist.

Conclusion

By describing these four qualities as "challenges," the Bishops are also recognizing that the portrait they offer is sadly not the experience for all too many people in today's society. Love, fidelity, intimacy are living qualities, tender shoots that properly tended will grow into a firm, strong, and fruitful relationship. What the Church says, by calling marriage a sacrament, is that couples are not and should not feel alone. We are one family, together in Christ!

Invitation to Share

Take a few moments of silence to reflect on the following questions. Then share your reflections.

1. To call marriage a "sacrament" is to see it as a window on God. What do I see through this window? (We can each share from our own life perspective.)
2. Look at the four qualities outlined in this Session:
   - — living faithfully
   - — giving life
   - — growing in mutuality
   - — taking time

   Share what these qualities mean for you, whatever your state in life. Focus on the one/s you feel you most need to nurture. What simple things would help me/us foster and nurture these four qualities?
3. The Church as family. The family as Church. In what ways could the Church be more like a family? In what ways can our family be "Church?" The sidebar on this page offers some key ideas around which you might build your sharing.

The Family as Church

"In our own time, in a world often alien and even hostile to faith, believing families are of primary importance as centers of living, radiant faith. For this reason the Second Vatican Council, using an ancient expression, calls the family the *Ecclesia domestica (Lumen Gentium*, 11). It is in the bosom of the family that parents are 'by word and example ... the first heralds of the faith with regard to their children. They should encourage them in the vocation which is proper to each child, fostering with special care any religious vocation' (*Lumen Gentium*, 11).

It is here that the father of the family, the mother, children, and all members of the family exercise the priesthood of the baptized in a privileged way 'by the reception of the sacraments, prayer and thanksgiving, the witness of a holy life, and self-denial and active charity' (*Lumen Gentium*, 10). Thus the home is the first school of Christian life and 'a school for human enrichment' (*Gaudium et Spes*, 52 §1). Here one learns endurance and the joy of work, fraternal love, generous–even repeated–forgiveness, and above all divine worship in prayer and the offering of one's life."

Catechism of the Catholic Church, 1656-7

INVITATION TO ACT

Sharing and being together in a small Christian community fosters growth in our faith and in our spirituality. However, no communal sharing is complete without a serious commitment to putting our faith into practice.

In this session we have reflected on our call to live in the light of Christ and to move away from the darkness: to what kind of action does this inspire us?

Some Suggestions

1. Build on your sharing discussion about the threats to family and marriage in today's secular society. Identify and commit to actions that will help people face these challenges. For example, what support could I/we be offering to people with troubled marriages? To single-parent families?
2. Build on your sharing discussion of the four qualities:
   — living faithfully
   — giving life
   — growing in mutuality
   — taking time

   (It may help to read the document on which this session's reflection is based: *Follow the Way of Love,* Pastoral Message of the U.S. Catholic Bishops [1994]. It provides reflection questions for each section. Available on the USCCB website: www.usccb.org/laity/follow.shtml).

   Commit to an action that will help foster these qualities both in your own family, and beyond. For example:

   — make mealtimes as a family more of a priority; begin them with a grace that celebrates who we are as family. Take time during this, once a week, for everyone to share the high point and the low point of their week

   — offer to babysit for a young couple, or a single parent, who do not have family in the area

   — establish a "homework" club for students who can't get the level of tutoring they need at home

— reach out to people who are socially isolated, and make a special effort to include them in family and/or community events

3. What are the unexpected difficulties encountered in marriage and in family life? What are the unexpected joys that marriage and life as a family can bring? Decide how this twofold experience can be put at the service of young couples, or those hoping to meet the "right" person, or of people preparing for marriage.
4. Arrange to view and then to discuss together the movie *Fireproof* (USCCB Rating: A-II [adults and adolescents]). For Catholic discussion guide resources, visit: www.fireproofmymarriage.com/catholics.php

Closing Prayer

Leader Let us pray that the love we have for one another may be a mirror of the love God has for us all.

Reader 1 For families who struggle to speak to one another in love:

All **Lord, be present in love.**

Reader 1 For families who enjoy being together:

All **Lord, be present in love.**

Reader 2 For those who are seeking their life's partner:

All **Lord, be present in love.**

Reader 2 For those who have found a companion on the road of life:

All **Lord, be present in love.**

Reader 3 For families who strive to live with less,
in order that others may have more:

All **Lord, be present in love.**

Reader 3 For families who are homeless,
or who go to bed hungry:

All **Lord, be present in love.**

Reader 4 For all God's children throughout the world,

All **Lord, be present in love.**

Leader Let us ask for God's blessings on ourselves and our loved ones.

All **May God, the almighty Father,**
give us joy and bless us.
May the only Son of God have mercy on us
and help us in good times and in bad.
May the Holy Spirit of God
always fill our hearts with love. Amen.

(Adapted from the final blessing, Rite of Marriage, *126)*

Suggested Song

I Have Loved You

or

Healer of Our Every Ill

(ARISE Songs for Season One CD, Track 2*)*

Looking Ahead

Prepare for the next faith-sharing meeting by reading over Session Five.

In particular:

- *Read the **"Focus for this Session"** (on page 57).*
- *Read the Gospel passage:* ***Luke 10:25-37***
- *Reread the "Key Themes of Catholic Social Teaching," on pages 77-79.* There is a brief (nine minutes) but compelling presentation of these key themes in Part One of the DVD *In the Footsteps of Christ* (USCCB Publication No 5-444; available online at www.usccbpublishing.org).

SESSION 5

Called to be Neighbor

> *What does the LORD require of you?*
> *To act justly, and to love mercy,*
> *and to walk humbly with your God."*

Micah 6:8

> *The Church is God's family in the world. In this family no one ought to go without the necessities of life. Yet at the same time* caritas-agape *[charity-love] extends beyond the frontiers of the Church. The parable of the Good Samaritan remains as a standard which imposes universal love towards the needy whom we encounter 'by chance' (cf. Luke 10:31), whoever they may be."*

Benedict XVI, *Deus Caritas Est*, 25b

Focus for this Session

- The Church's tradition of charity is as essential as preaching the Word and celebrating the sacraments
- New challenge from development of industrial society
- True charity takes justice into account
- Bringing the faith perspective to charity and justice
- The Church as "community of love"

GATHER

Opening Prayer

Leader Let us spend a few moments,
becoming more aware of God's presence ...
... God's presence in us and in this community,
gathered in Jesus' name.

Pause for a few moments of quiet.

9

Suggested Song

Lead Me, Lord

or

God Is Love *(ARISE Songs for Season One* CD, Track 13*)*

Then one member of the group reads the following prayer:

Almighty and ever-living God,
empower your one human family to join hands
on our journey of faith.
Send us your Spirit of hope,
so that we may work
to alleviate human suffering
and foster charity and justice
in our world.

All **Amen.**

(*From* Being Neighbor: The Catechism and Social Justice, *USCCB, April, 1998)*

Living our Faith

Share briefly your experience of putting into effect the action you chose after the last session.

BREAKING OPEN OUR STORY

Reflection

If you were to travel to Paris, France, Notre Dame Cathedral would probably be on your list of places to visit. Seen through the eyes of faith, this impressive building could be viewed as a sermon in stone. Near the Cathedral you would find a building that has a remarkable name: the Hôtel-Dieu, literally the "God-Hostel."

The Hôtel-Dieu was founded in 651 by the then Bishop of Paris (Saint Landry), as an institution to care for the poor and the sick. It offered food, shelter, and medical care. If Notre Dame stands as testimony to faith as service to God, then the Hôtel-Dieu stands as testimony to faith as service to humanity, the "stranger," the hungry, the poor. This, the Bishop decided, was the appropriate pastoral way to continue the Church's tradition of offering charity and hospitality. It is one of Europe's oldest hospitals and still operating today. Of course, the original, small building is long gone, but, through the centuries, it has always been replaced—and its original religious nature is remembered in its name.

Charity: an "essential"

As the Church spread, "the exercise of charity became established as one of her essential activities, along with the administration of the sacraments and the proclamation of the word: love for widows and orphans, prisoners, and the sick and needy of every kind, is as essential to her as the ministry of the sacraments and preaching of the Gospel. The Church cannot neglect the service of charity any more than she can neglect the Sacraments and the Word."

Benedict XVI, *Deus Caritas Est*, 22

We can take pride that many of the institutions and social systems of today, such as hospitals, schools, and social service agencies began as pastoral initiatives by the Church (and it would be remiss not to acknowledge the huge contribution to this made by women, both lay and Religious). The impulse for this outreach was to put into effect the values of the Gospel, above all the great command to love. Quite simply, this was following in the footsteps of Christ.

In the past couple of hundred years, particularly in view of the huge changes in economic and social structures in the 19th century, and the new forms of poverty they spawned, it became clear that what had become conventional forms of "charity" were inadequate. This led some (Karl Marx, for example) to go so far as to condemn "charity" as demeaning to the poor, not just as a way for the rich to salve their consciences, but as a way to preserve their own status and rob the poor of their rights.

The Church's answer was more balanced, rejecting any caricature of charity: "Charity will never be true charity unless it takes justice into account ... let no one attempt with small gifts of charity to exempt himself from the great duties imposed by justice" (Pius XI, *Divini Redemptoris,* 59 [quoted in *Economic Justice for All,* 120]). Over the century since Leo XIII there have been many papal messages, developing Catholic social teaching. At their heart lie fundamental guidelines that are valid not just for Catholics, but for everyone seriously concerned with humanity and for the world in which we live. Key to this is getting the balance right between the necessary commitment to justice and the ministry of charity.

The Church teaches that justice is why we have what we call "politics"—not in the party sense, but meaning the way people as citizens can and should get together to organize the stuff of common life for the common good.

Benedict XVI signals, though, that, as Christians, our sense of justice should be colored by the Word of God. We bring the faith perspective to justice, a perspective that says the way we choose to regulate our lives should match God's dream for humanity, for the common good. This is a spiritual dimension that "purifies" our vision of justice. It liberates justice from ideological manipulation. It prevents us being blinded by the dazzling effect of power and special interests. In part this will mean acknowledging when we ourselves are part of systems that are unjust, and accepting to change ourselves.

True Charity

"It is imperative that the freedom and dignity of the person being helped be respected with the utmost consideration, that the purity of one's charitable intentions be not stained by seeking one's own advantage or by striving for domination, and especially that the demands of justice be satisfied lest the giving of what is due in justice be represented as the offering of a charitable gift. Not only the effects but also the causes of these ills must be removed and the help be given in such a way that the recipients may gradually be freed from dependence on outsiders and become self-sufficient."

Apostolicam Actuositatem, 8
Vatican II Decree
on the Apostolate of the Laity

"Love—*caritas*—will always prove necessary, even in the most just society. There is no ordering of the State so just that it can eliminate the need for a service of love.... There will always be suffering which cries out for consolation and help. There will always be loneliness. There will always be situations of material need where help in the form of concrete love of neighbor is indispensable" (*Deus Caritas Est*, 28b).

The early Church concerned itself with making love real for no other reason than it made Christ present. This is why "charity" stands alongside preaching the Word and celebrating the sacraments as one of the Church's essential activities. It is part of who the Church is, "a community of love."

But we should note that charity did not stand alone: it was charity because it was fed by the Word of God; it was charity because in the liturgy the people turned in prayer asking, in Jesus' name, God to be present, to strengthen and to console them in their work.

This is the fuller vision of charity founded on a different vision of what is "due" to people, founded on their inalienable dignity as daughters and sons of God, sisters and brothers in Christ, and called to live one day in community with God for ever. By our charity, we say to whoever needs it ***"ARISE!"***

Invitation to Share

Take a few moments of silence to reflect on the following question. Then share your reflections.

1. When did the Word of God prompt me to respond in charity and justice?
2. Share ways in which you think God's justice makes different demands on us than does ordinary justice.
3. Share your ideas for what would count as the distinguishing characteristics of true charity. Part of this could be sharing examples of both what you think counts as "true" charity; and examples of superficial "charity."

BREAKING OPEN GOD'S STORY

The Word of God

Sometime before the meeting, the leader asks a member of the group to be prepared to proclaim the passage from the Gospel according to Luke.

Luke 10:25-37

The Parable of the Good Samaritan

Reader *The Gospel of the Lord.*

All **Praise to you, Lord Jesus Christ.**

Reflect

Moment of silent reflection

What word, phrase, or image from the Scripture reading touches my heart or speaks to my life?

Invitation to Share

The leader invites those who so wish to echo a key word or phrase that touched them from the Scripture passage.

REFLECTION

Today's Gospel passage gives us a character who has passed into everyday speech. A search on the web for "Good Samaritan" offers over 3.5 million potential sites. In an age before computers and printing, the parable was clearly and colorfully presented in many of the stained-glass windows of cathedrals in medieval Europe.

We could all probably retell the essentials of the story without having to look it up in our Bibles. However, our familiarity with it may lead us to overlook the different levels of meaning that lie there, waiting to be discovered.

At the heart of the passage lies a great story of solidarity. Like the team who built the house in session one, this is about recognizing a need, being deeply moved to compassion, and then acting in a firm and determined way to help. It is not just a quick fix: the Good Samaritan goes beyond the band-aid, making sure that the victim receives ongoing care (entrusting him to the care of the inn-keeper), despite the expense, and open-endedly commits to whatever it may cost.

What the Good Samaritan did is rightly held up as an example of charity. In the parable as Jesus tells it, however, there are *three* characters. As well as the Samaritan, there is the priest and the Levite. The priest and the Levite, precisely because of their religious positions, should have been "good" by definition. By contrast, in cultural terms, the Samaritan is doubly "bad." Firstly, he is a foreigner, an alien; secondly, he is a heretic, worse than a heathen. In session one we saw Christ among us on the road from Jerusalem as the "stranger"; today we see Christ upholding the example of a "stranger" in both nationality and in religion, on the road from Jerusalem ...

Take today's complete story, and it also becomes a challenge to examine where we might be failing justice, God's justice. The priest and the Levite come out of this story badly not because they were not following whatever Roman law may have been in force at the time, but precisely because their sense of justice should have been informed by the heart of *Torah*, the timeless Law of God: love God, love your neighbor.

Martin Luther King, Jr., took the road from Jerusalem to Jericho and describes the 17 miles or so as winding, steep, and treacherous, an ideal place for attacks and robbery. Thinking about that led Doctor King to suggest the following interpretation of today's parable: "It is not enough to aid a wounded man on the Jericho Road; it is also important to change the conditions which make robbery possible. Philanthropy is commendable, but it must not cause the philanthropist to overlook the circumstances of economic injustice which make philanthropy necessary."

Charity and justice are subtly intermingled in today's Gospel. The Good Samaritan succeeded in charity; the priest and Levite failed in justice. The dividing line between them in modern day life can be just as blurred. What is certain is that both are needed: "Catholic teaching calls us to serve those in need and to change the structures that deny people their dignity and rights as children of God. Service and action, charity and justice are complementary components of parish social ministry. Neither alone is sufficient; both are essential signs of the Gospel at work" (*Communities of Salt and Light*, USCCB 1994).

There is no better model for charity than the Good Samaritan, who clearly gave without counting the cost. "The Christian's program—the program of the Good Samaritan, the program of Jesus—is a 'heart that sees.' This heart sees where love is needed and acts accordingly" (Benedict XVI, *Deus Caritas Est*, 32b).

Working for justice may cost us in a different way. It involves questioning the status quo, the established structures, as Jesus does in today's Gospel. The trouble is, because we ourselves are part of these structures, we are liable to have blind spots—as did the priest and the Levite. We simply cannot claim we are walking in the footsteps of Christ, and then pass by on the other side.

Did you notice that Jesus never does answer the question, "Who is my neighbor?" Instead he offers an alternative question: "How have you shown yourself to be a good neighbor to others?" In our final session we'll discover yet another dimension to proving ourselves a good neighbor ...

Prayer urgently needed

"Prayer, as a means of drawing ever new strength from Christ, is concretely and urgently needed. People who pray are not wasting their time, even though the situation appears desperate and seems to call for action alone. Piety does not undermine the struggle against the poverty of our neighbors, however extreme."

Benedict XVI, *Deus Caritas Est*, 36

Invitation to Share

Take a few moments of silence to reflect on the following questions. Then share your reflections.

1. Share about someone who has a "heart that sees"; someone who "sees where love is needed and acts accordingly."
2. If Christ were to retell the parable today, for our country or state, who might the three characters be? Who might I be in the story? What does this prompt me to do?

3. Reflect together on the social concerns ministry offered by your parish. Are we, as a community, proving to be a good neighbor both to members of our parish and to those in the wider community? What could we do to improve and/or expand this social ministry?
4. What is one justice issue that I would like to work on that I believe would promote greater solidarity? What steps will I take in the coming week to start that?

INVITATION TO ACT

Sharing and being together in a small Christian community fosters growth in our faith and in our spirituality. But no communal sharing is complete without a serious commitment to putting our faith into practice.

In this session we have reflected on what is means to be "neighbor": to what kind of action does this inspire us?

Some Suggestions

1. Be a voice for the poor and homeless at community meetings. Write or email local and national leaders regarding these and other concerns for the poor and disadvantaged.
2. Build on your sharing as to what counts as "true" charity, and commit to an action this week that matches those criteria. For example, assist at a shelter for the homeless, a soup kitchen, or a food bank in your area.
3. Build on your sharing about the social concerns ministry offered in your parish, and commit to building this. For example, if the parish does not already have a social ministry committee, a peace and justice committee, take steps to initiate one. If one already exists, commit to offering concrete help to an existing parish initiative. Invite the whole parish to support these ministries by their prayer, include them regularly in the Sunday Prayer of the Faithful.

4. Commit to reading *Strangers No More: Together on the Journey of Hope* (Pastoral Letter Concerning Migration from the Catholic Bishops of Mexico and the United States). It is available on the USCCB website: www.usccb.org/mrs/stranger.shtml
5. Arrange to view and then to discuss together the movie *The Visitor* (USCCB Rating: A-III [Adults]).

CLOSING PRAYER

Leader God our loving Father,
fill us with the power of your Holy Spirit
so that, our hearts may be filled
with the spirit of true charity,
we will be strengthened to be neighbor
to all who are in need.
We ask this through Christ, your Son,
who showed your love for all.

All **Amen.**

Suggested Song

The Harvest of Justice

or

We Are the Light of the World
(ARISE Songs for Season One CD, Track 7*)*

or

Blest Are They *(ARISE Songs for Season One* CD, Track 8*)*

Looking Ahead

Prepare for the next faith-sharing meeting by reading over Session Six.

In particular:

- *read the **"Focus for this Session"** (on page 67).*
- *Read the Gospel passage: **Matthew 25:31-46**. It may help to set this passage in context if you were to read all of chapters 24 and 25: This covers what Matthew presents as Jesus' fifth and final sermon.*
- *Reread the "Key Themes of Catholic Social Teaching," on pages 77-79.*

SESSION 6

Called to ARISE!

There are those whose being is possession. There are those whose essence is giving."

"Lord, try us" by Helder Camara

Love of God and love of neighbor have become one: in the least of the brethren we find Jesus himself, and in Jesus we find God."

Benedict XVI, *Deus Caritas Est*, 15

"It is by what they have done for the poor that Jesus Christ will recognize his chosen ones (cf. Matthew 25:31-36)."

Catechism of the Catholic Church, 2443

Focus for this Session

- The poor, hungry, thirsty, homeless, and prisoners are "sacraments" of Christ
- The mark of true disciples of Christ is what they do for the poor
- The implications of our belief in the Incarnation: God made present in human history

GATHER

Opening Prayer

Leader All-powerful God,
increase our strength of will for doing good
that Christ may find an eager welcome
at his coming
and call us to his side in the kingdom of heaven,
where he lives and reigns with you
and the Holy Spirit,
one God, for ever and ever.

All **Amen.**

Opening Prayer, First Sunday of Advent, *Roman Missal*

Suggested Song

The Cry of the Poor

Living Our Faith

Share briefly your experience of putting into effect the action you chose after the last session.

BREAKING OPEN OUR STORY

Reflection

In session two we saw how Christ's proclamation of Scripture was welcomed in his own town synagogue, but when he began to talk about the implications of fulfilling what Scripture said, it aroused hostility and even a death threat. It still happens that when people in the Church speak out prophetically, some feel threatened and try to silence the message by quashing the messenger.

Bishop Skylstad of Spokane, Washington, narrates an experience of the prophetic power that speaking out in the service of God's justice can have.

"A few years ago I had the opportunity of visiting the country of Malawi as a board member for Catholic Relief Services (CRS). Shortly after arriving in the country, CRS staff members made me aware of a relatively brief pastoral letter by the bishops of that country, *Living Our Faith*, issued at the beginning of Lent in 1992. The bishops talked about dignity and unity of humankind, the aspiration to greater equality and unity, participation in all of public life, and a system of justice that works fairly. Almost immediately after the letter was issued, the bishops were thrown into prison, scheduled to be executed. If it hadn't been for the diplomatic community, their lives probably would not have been spared. Malawi's then president for life was extremely angry. New elections were called for, and he was voted out of office. I saw from a distance, too, the three luxurious residential palaces he built in a country that is one of the poorest in Africa. They were huge edifices.

While I was meeting with some parishioners in the city of Mzuzu in the northern part of Malawi, one of the ladies told me: 'You can't believe how our country has changed. We still have problems, but things are so much better now. It's wonderful!' One of the Sisters observed that everyone knows what a tremendous impact the bishops had made with their teaching. What a remarkable transformation was brought about in that society by the courage of those seven bishops!"

We who live in democracies are used to free speech, and if we were to read what the Malawi bishops said, we might find it rather tame. However, it is clear that the Bishops of Malawi read the signs of the times in their own country, and as Bishop Skylstad says, they "spoke to the moment." As a result they effected a change, not just in the thinking of Catholics, but in their lives; not just in the lives of Catholics, but the lives of everyone, Christian or non-Christian, in Malawi. Saint Augustine once said: "With you I am a Christian, for you I am a bishop." The Malawi Bishops clearly spoke as Bishops, as Catholics—but also as citizens and as human beings. This, of course, is the real meaning of "catholic" ...

Invitation to Share

Take a few moments of silence to reflect on one of the following questions. Then share your reflections.

1. If you had to write a pastoral letter, what would you write about? (What situation would you highlight, what action would you propose, and what part of the Church's teaching would you use to do that?) Would you be willing to go to prison for what you had written?
2. Share an experience of a Church document, or a Gospel passage, that has influenced your understanding, or your attitude toward an issue, and/or encouraged you to make an action response in faith.
3. Share an example of someone that you would describe as either speaking out or living out the message of the Gospel in a "prophetic" way.

BREAKING OPEN GOD'S STORY

The Word of God

Sometime before the meeting, the leader asks a member of the group to be prepared to proclaim the passage from from the Gospel according to Matthew.

Matthew 25:31-46

"Just as you did it to one of the least of these, you did it to me."

Reader *The Gospel of the Lord.*

All **Praise to you, Lord Jesus Christ.**

Reflection

Moment of silent reflection

- What word, phrase, or image from the Scripture reading touches my heart or speaks to my life?

Invitation to Share

The leader invites those who so wish to echo a key word or phrase that touched them from the Scripture passage.

Reflection

"The Greatest Teacher" was the title of the session in Season One where we reflected on the portrait of Jesus that is presented by the Gospel of Matthew. In today's Scripture, again from Matthew, we have just heard the Teacher's last class, his final teaching. The very next verse begins the account of Jesus' passion and death. This gives an added poignancy to the text, projecting it beyond Jesus' death (and resurrection) to his return in glory.

It is the very vivid parable of the Last Judgment: the blessed who are welcomed into God's kingdom; and the cursed who are sent to eternal punishment. For each person, the "evidence" that Christ offers at their "trial" is the same: feeding the hungry; giving drink to the thirsty; welcoming the stranger; clothing the naked; visiting the sick and the imprisoned.

Commenting on this passage, the U.S. Bishops' *Pastoral Economic Justice for All* invites us to notice how "neither the blessed nor the cursed are astounded that they are judged by the Son of Man, nor that judgment is rendered according to the works of charity. The shock comes when they find that in neglecting the poor, the outcast, the oppressed, they were rejecting Jesus himself" (*Economic Justice for All*, 40).

Both the blessed and the cursed clearly know what justice and charity demand. What makes the difference is that the blessed knew how, where, and when these principles should be applied to the reality of everyday life. Above all, to whom. The U. S. Bishops invite us to link this with our fundamental belief in the Incarnation: "Jesus who came as 'Emmanuel' (God-with-us, Matthew 1:23) and who promises to be with his people until the end of the age (Matthew 28:20) is hidden in those most in need; to reject them is to reject God made manifest in history" (*Economic Justice for All*, 40).

Serving Christ in those in need—this is the mark of the true disciple. Jesus had already said the measure of the true disciple is not that someone calls him "Lord", (see Matthew 7:21-23). True disciples are those who do the will of the Father. The "to do" list that we saw in session two, setting out the mission we share with Jesus, becomes the measure against which we will be judged.

This has enormous implications for the way we should regard solidarity, social change, and "this world." If Christ identifies himself with the poor, hungry, thirsty, homeless, then where they are, he is. In them, too, today's parable tells us, is our salvation. The poor and the needy are nothing less than sacraments. Through them, Christ tells us, we have his presence; through them, Christ promises, we will find salvation. This is not some "other world" promise made to the poor. Christ could not be clearer in building the promise of eternal life in "this world."

How are we to answer that call in practice today? This faith-sharing resource cannot give the answer. These words may not be read until months, years after they were written. What ***ARISE*** can do is help persuade you to live with the question. As Catholics we have the resources of a tradition we call the social teaching of the Church. This tradition clearly sets out the principles and values that we can use to analyze the here and now of our situation, so that we can discern appropriate responses.

We might try to excuse ourselves from this task of discernment: "I haven't got time to study all the pros and cons of this issue..." "Economics nowadays is far too complicated ..." Indeed, our modern world is complex. In the life of faith, as in ordinary life, we can turn to expert help. The key local reference in this shared task of discernment is our bishop; it is an essential part of his ministry as bishop, that he expresses as a solemn promise during his episcopal ordination (see sidebar). Especially in questions of

Bishop's promise to be welcoming and merciful to the poor

"In the rite of episcopal ordination, prior to the act of consecration itself, the candidate must respond to several questions which express the essential elements of his office and recall the duties of his future ministry. He promises expressly to be, in the Lord's name, welcoming and merciful to the poor and to all those in need of consolation and assistance (see the *Rite of Ordination of a Bishop*, 43)."

Benedict XVI, *Deus Caritas Est,* 32

social teaching, our bishops collaborate to provide guidance through national statements. Our bishops also provide the launch pad for action through their official agencies (see page 30). However, these agencies exist to channel our action, not simply to act on our behalf. In today's parable of the Last Judgment, no one is excused on the grounds "I thought someone else was supposed to be doing that ..."

If I were accused and brought to trial for "being a Christian," would there be enough evidence to convict me?

Invitation to Share

Take a few moments of silence to reflect on one of the following questions. Then share your reflections.

1. If I had to retell the Last Judgment parable for today's world, what kind of action toward what kind of people would I list? (See one example, by Dorothy Day, in the sidebar.)
2. Reread the "evidence" that Jesus offers in today's parable. Share your experiences of offering or of receiving help in these ways. What are the agencies in our parish and in our diocese that I found helped me live out my faith in a way that matches today's Gospel?
3. What might we be able to do as a response to today's Gospel passage as a group that would be more difficult alone? What can our group do to spread the message of this Gospel in our parish, and encourage others to work with us for solidarity?

If Christ told the parable today ...

"We are the rich man of the world, and the poor man is at the gate, and we are afraid the day is coming when God will say,

'Depart from me, accursed ones, into the everlasting fire which was prepared for the devil and his angels.

For I was hungry and you polluted the earth with your mines and your bombs and wars which starved the poor; I was thirsty, and you contaminated even the ocean and the waters of the earth with your hydrogen bombs; I was a stranger, and you made agreements with former allies who now are enemies, to keep me in displaced persons' camps to this day, and daily you make more homeless; naked, and you make weapons and profits for the rich and the poor have not the clothes to cover them; I was sick and in prison, and my numbers ever increased.'"

Dorothy Day, *The Catholic Worker,* January 1957

INVITATION TO ACT

Sharing and being together in a small Christian community fosters growth in our faith and in our spirituality. However, no communal sharing is complete without a serious commitment to putting our faith into practice.

The poor are the treasure of the Church

"... the case of the deacon Lawrence (†258). The dramatic description of Lawrence's martyrdom was known to Saint Ambrose (†397) and it provides a fundamentally authentic picture of the saint. As the one responsible for the care of the poor in Rome, Lawrence had been given a period of time, after the capture of the Pope and of Lawrence's fellow deacons, to collect the treasures of the Church and hand them over to the civil authorities. He distributed to the poor whatever funds were available and then presented to the authorities the poor themselves as the real treasure of the Church."

Benedict XVI, *Deus Caritas Est*, 23.

In this session we have reflected on the qualities of a true disciple: to what kind of action does this inspire us?

Some Suggestions

1. Find out about local initiatives such as food banks, soup kitchens, clothing banks, hospital and prison visiting. Help and/or promote their activity in some active way. Become involved.
2. Choose an issue that is of concern today, in your town, parish, or diocese. Commit yourself to reading up about that issue, especially what your bishop or the U.S. Bishops say. (You may find it helps to do this as group, each person committing to read and then share their learnings from a different document.) Let what you learn from this touch your heart, and prompt you to action. For example, send a letter/email to your local and national representatives in defense of the poor, the homeless ...
3. Share with family and friends your experience of these six weeks of Season Three of ***ARISE.*** Invite a friend, neighbor, or family member to join your ***ARISE*** group for Season Four (Lent).

Closing Prayer

Gather for prayer around one single large candle.
This should be the only source of light.
As each reader pronounces a task, they light a
smaller candle from the main candle.
Arrange it so that by the end of the litany, everyone
has a lighted candle.

Leader We are called to follow in the footsteps of Christ.
At times we may feel we stumble in the dark;
yet we know that Christ,
who is the way and the light,
walks with us.
Let us invoke the Spirit
who empowered Jesus to fulfill his mission,
so that we too may bring light to our world today.

Members of the group take it in turn to read aloud:

Reader 1 The Spirit of the Lord is upon me, ...
Light small candle from the main candle
... because he has anointed me
and sent me to give food to the hungry.
Pause

Reader 2 The Spirit of the Lord is upon me, ...
Light small candle from the main candle
... because he has anointed me
and sent me to give drink to the thirsty.
Pause

Reader 3 The Spirit of the Lord is upon me, ...
Light small candle from the main candle
... because he has anointed me
and sent me to welcome the stranger.
Pause

Reader 4 The Spirit of the Lord is upon me, ...
Light small candle from the main candle
... because he has anointed me
and sent me to clothe the naked.
Pause

Reader 5 The Spirit of the Lord is upon me, ...
Light small candle from the main candle
... because he has anointed me
and sent me to take care of the sick.
Pause

Reader 6 The Spirit of the Lord is upon me, ...
Light small candle from the main candle
... because he has anointed me
and sent me to visit those in prison.
Pause

All **God our loving Father,**
keep your Church alert in faith
to the signs of the times
and eager to accept the challenge of the Gospel.
Open our hearts to the needs of all humanity,
so that sharing their grief and anguish,
their joy and hope,
we may faithfully bring them
the Good News of your salvation
and advance together
on the way to your kingdom.
We ask this Christ our Lord.
Amen.

Leader Let us each take our candles home,
and place them where they will remind us
that we are called to follow in Christ's footsteps.
Let us light the candle,
particularly on days of darkness,
and pray simply:
"Christ our light, be with me.
Help me to see and serve you in others."

Concluding Song

Suggested Song

Whatsoever You Do

or

Christ Be Our Light

(ARISE Songs for Season One CD, Track 15*)*

Appendix
Key Themes of Catholic Social Teaching
Reflections of the U.S Catholic Bishops

The Church's social teaching is a rich treasure of wisdom about building a just society and living lives of holiness amidst the challenges of modern society. Modern Catholic social teaching has been articulated through a tradition of papal, conciliar, and episcopal documents. The depth and richness of this tradition can be understood best through a direct reading of these documents. In these brief reflections, we highlight several of the key themes that are at the heart of our Catholic social tradition.

Life and Dignity of the Human Person

The Catholic Church proclaims that human life is sacred and that the dignity of the human person is the foundation of a moral vision for society. This belief is the foundation of all the principles of our social teaching. In our society, human life is under direct attack from abortion and euthanasia. The value of human life is being threatened by cloning, embryonic stem cell research, and the use of the death penalty. Catholic teaching also calls on us to work to avoid war. Nations must protect the right to life by finding increasingly effective ways to prevent conflicts and resolve them by peaceful means. We believe that every person is precious, that people are more important than things, and that the measure of every institution is whether it threatens or enhances the life and dignity of the human person.

Call to Family, Community, and Participation

The person is not only sacred but also social. How we organize our society in economics and politics, in law and policy directly affects human dignity and the capacity of individuals to grow in community. Marriage and the family are the central social institutions that must be supported and strengthened, not undermined. We believe people have a right and a duty to participate in society, seeking together the common good and well-being of all, especially the poor and vulnerable.

Rights and Responsibilities

The Catholic tradition teaches that human dignity can be protected and a healthy community can be achieved only if human rights are protected and responsibilities are met. Therefore, every person has a fundamental right to life and a right to those things required for human decency. Corresponding to these rights are duties and responsibilities—to one another, to our families, and to the larger society.

Option for the Poor and Vulnerable

A basic moral test is how our most vulnerable members are faring. In a society marred by deepening divisions between rich and poor, our tradition recalls the story of the Last Judgment (Matthew 25:31-46) and instructs us to put the needs of the poor and vulnerable first.

The Dignity of Work and the Rights of Workers

The economy must serve people, not the other way around. Work is more than a way to make a living; it is a form of continuing participation in God's creation. If the dignity of work is to be protected, then the basic rights of workers must be respected—the right to productive work, to decent and fair wages, to the organization and joining of unions, to private property, and to economic initiative.

Solidarity

We are one human family whatever our national, racial, ethnic, economic, and ideological differences. We are our brothers' and sisters' keepers, wherever they may be. Loving our neighbor has global dimensions in a shrinking world. At the core of the virtue of solidarity is the pursuit of justice and peace. Pope Paul VI taught that "if you want peace, work for justice" (Paul VI, For the Celebration of the Day of Peace [January 1, 1972]). The Gospel calls us to be peacemakers. Our love for all our sisters and brothers demands that we promote peace in a world surrounded by violence and conflict.

Care for God's Creation

We show our respect for the Creator by our stewardship of creation. Care for the earth is not just an Earth Day slogan, it is a requirement of our faith. We are called to protect people and the planet, living our faith in relationship with all of God's creation. This environmental challenge has fundamental moral and ethical dimensions that cannot be ignored.

This summary should only be a starting point for those interested in Catholic social teaching. A full understanding can only be achieved by reading the papal, conciliar, and episcopal documents that make up this rich tradition. The complete text of *Sharing Catholic Social Teaching: Challenges and Directions* is available online at www.usccb.org/sdwp/projects/socialteaching/socialteaching.shtml

Text is drawn from *Sharing Catholic Social Teaching: Challenges and Directions* (Washington, DC: USCCB, 1998) and *Forming Consciences for Faithful Citizenship: A Call to Political Responsibility from the Catholic Bishops of the United States* (Washington DC: USCCB, 2007); available on www.faithfulcitizenship.org

Music Resources

Alphabetical Index of Suggested Songs

Christ Be Beside Me
Words, based on St Patrick's Breastplate: James D. Quinn, S.J.
© James D. Quinn, S.J. Selah Publishing Co. Inc., agent.
Music: Scottish traditional (Bunessan)

God Has Chosen Me
Words and music: Bernadette Farrell
© 1990 Bernadette Farrell. Published by OCP Publications

I Have Loved You
Words, based on Jeremiah 31:3, Psalm 24:3, and music: Michael Joncas
© 1979 OCP Publications

Lead Me, Lord
Words, based on Matthew 5:3-12, 7:7, John 14:6, and music: John D. Becker
© 1987 John D. Becker. Published by OCP Publications

One Bread, One Body
Words, from 1 Corinthians 10:16, 17:2-4, Galatians 3:28, and the *Didaché*, and music: John Foley, S.J.
© 1978 John Foley, S.J. and OCP Publications

Take the Word of God with You
Words: James Harrison © 1991 James Harrison
Music: Christopher Walker © 1991 Christopher Walker.
Published by OCP Publications

The Cry of the Poor
Words, based on Psalm 34:2-3, 6-7, 18-19, 23, and music: John Foley, S.J.
© 1978, 1990 John Foley, S.J., and OCP Publications

The Harvest of Justice
Words, based on Philippians 1:11, Leviticus 19:9, 23:22, and music: David Haas
© 1985 GIA Publications, Inc.

We Are Many Parts
Words, based on 1 Corinthians 12, 13, and music: Marty Haugen
© 1980, 1986 GIA Publications, Inc.

We Walk by Faith
Words: Henry Alford (18140-71), alt.
Music: Marty Haugen
© 1984 GIA Publications, Inc.

Whatsoever You Do
Words, based on Matthew 5:3-12 and 25:34-36, and music: Willard F. Jabusch.
Administered by OCP Publications

When Love Is Found
Words: Brian Wren © Hope Publishing Co.
Music: English traditional ("O waly, waly")

All of the songs listed above are on the *In the Footsteps of Christ CD*, one sample of which is part of every ***ARISE*** *Parish Kit*. For further information, including how to order additional copies, see page 84.

The details of other songs, suggested in the sessions but already included on the *Encounter with Christ CD* (***ARISE*** *Songs for Season One*) can be found in *Encounter with Christ* (the faith-sharing book for Season One), pages 69-70.

Most of the songs suggested for the sessions can be found in the standard hymnals or parish worship aids. Should you want to get in touch with any of the publishers of the songs suggested (for example, to obtain printed copies of the music scores, or to purchase downloadable PDF, TIFF, or MP3 files, or to ask for permission to reprint copyright words), here are their contact details.

GIA Publications, Inc.
7404 South Mason Avenue
Chicago, IL 60638
Phone: 800-442-1358 or 708-496-3800
Fax: 708-496-3828
Website: www.giamusic.com
Email: custserv@giamusic.com
For downloadable copies (as PDF or TIFF files, with preview and listen options): www.hymnprint.net

Hope Publishing Company
380 South Main Place
Carol Stream, IL 60188
Phone: 800-323-1049
Fax: 630-665-2552
Website: www.hopepublishing.com
Email: hope@hopepublishing.com
Permissions processed through www.OneLicense.net

Oregon Catholic Press Publications (OCP)
5536 NE Hassalo
Portland, OR 97213
Phone: 800-LITURGY (548-8749)
Fax: 800-4-OCP-FAX (462-7329)
Website: www.ocp.org
Email: liturgy@ocp.org
Permissions processed through www.LicenSingonline.org
For downloadable copies in PDF and GIF format: www.printandpraise.com

Selah Publishing Co. Inc.
PO Box 98066
Pittsburgh, PA 15227
Phone: 800-852-6172
Fax: 412-886-1022
Email: customerservice@selahpub.com
Permissions processed through www.LicenSingonline.org *or through* www.OneLicense.net

ARISE Resources

The five Seasons of faith sharing in small Christian communities are central to the ***ARISE Together in Christ*** process.

For each Season, RENEW International offers a **faith-sharing book,** a **music CD** with the songs suggested in the faith-sharing book, and a Seasonal Supplement to the ***ARISE*** *Liturgy Handbook,* offering pastoral notes and practical suggestions on how to link the process with the Sunday celebration of the Eucharist.

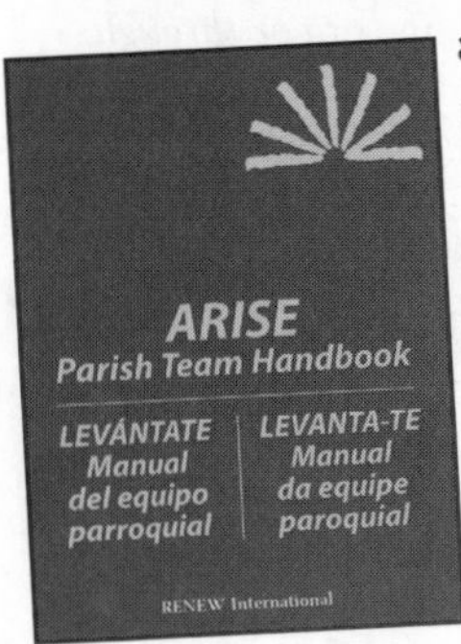

The five Seasons are:

Season One	**Encountering Christ Today**
Season Two	**Change Our Hearts**
Season Three	**In the Footsteps of Christ**
Season Four	**New Heart, New Spirit**
Season Five	**We Are the Good News!**

The faith-sharing books are designed principally for use by adults; however, they are complemented by materials for children and for youth. Both are designed around the same themes and the same Scripture passages as in the adult books.

ARISE for youth

Faith-sharing materials for each session of all five Seasons, written especially for youth (Grades 10-12). Also includes a separate ***ARISE*** for youth Leader Guide.

ARISE Family Sharing Pages

A friendly easy way to explore the same faith themes at home and in class. Four-page, full color worksheet for each session of each Season. Available for Grades 1-3, and Grades 4-6.

There are additional resources designed to foster the fruitful implementation of *ARISE, WHY CATHOLIC?,* and, any faith-sharing process:

SOWING SEEDS
Essentials for Small Community Leaders

This book offers a comprehensive collection of pastoral insights and practical suggestions to help small community leaders guide their groups in a way that nourishes spiritual growth. Culled from RENEW International's three decades of experience in pioneering and promoting small Christian communities, this book overflows with simple but effective ideas and strategies that will enhance the way these groups reflect on and respond to the Gospel.

GLEANINGS
A Personal Prayer Journal

Many participants in small communities tell us how much they are helped in both their shared discussion and their personal reflection by the technique known as journaling: keeping a notebook for the expression of thoughts and ideas.

Gleanings is a valuable tool for both avid and occasional journal writers. Each page spread is decorated with a spiritual quotation or musing that can inspire prayerful reflection on your relationship with God. The comfortably-sized format makes it an excellent companion for your personal faith journey, helping tap into the richness of God's wisdom within you. It is also a thoughtful gift for friends or family.

For more information or to order, please visit our secure online bookstore at **www.renewintl.org/store** or use our toll free order line: 1-888-433-3221.

Between Seasons of ***ARISE***, small communities who want to keep up a regular rhythm of faith-sharing can use the following:

PrayerTime Cycle A, B, C: Faith-Sharing Reflections on the Sunday Gospels

This faith-sharing resource responds to the U.S. Bishops' suggestion that "every parish meeting can begin with the reading of the upcoming Sunday's Gospel, followed by a time of reflection and faith sharing."

With each Sunday's Gospel as a focus, *PrayerTime* proposes meaningful reflections, focused faith-sharing questions, related questions for consideration, and prayers as a source of spiritual nourishment and inspiration.

Use *PrayerTime* any time of year, whenever the small community needs. It is recommended *PrayerTime* be employed by groups between seasons of ***ARISE,*** especially after Easter and during the summer. It is also ideal for beginning meetings of the pastoral council, staff, and other parish groups. The themes can also be read personally as a way to prepare for Sunday Mass.

This invaluable resource is also available in Spanish:

Oremos Ciclo A, B, C Reflexiones sobre los Evangelios Domincales para Compartir la Fe

LONGING FOR THE HOLY: Spirituality for Everyday Life

Based on selected insights of Ronald Rolheiser, O.M.I.

Experience how the gentle spiritual guidance and practical wisdom of best-selling Catholic author Fr. Ronald Rolheiser, O.M.I. can enliven everyday life. Suitable for small community faith sharing or individual reflection, *Longing for the Holy* covers different dimensions of contemporary spiritual life for those who want to enrich their sense of the presence of God and develop a deeper spirituality.

The Participant's Book contains twelve sessions with prayers, reflections, sharing questions, and stories from saints and contemporary people of faith.

This resource is also available as a **four CD-set audio edition,** which has both narrated text and songs for all twelve sessions.

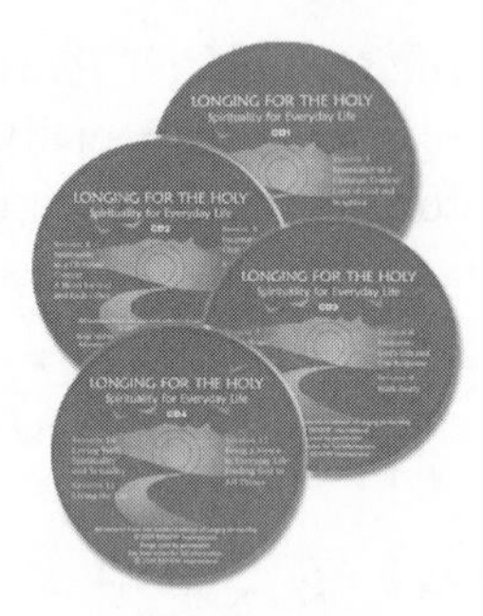

The songs suggested for the moments of prayer in the faith-sharing sessions are offered on this 13-song anthology CD.

The Kit includes the essential ingredients to bring this engaging spiritual experience to your parish or small Christian community. Purchase of the kit provides membership benefits including the opportunity for web-based workshops and faith enrichment experiences, as well as a web library of support materials.

Strengthen Your Faith with

WHY CATHOLIC? Journey through the Catechism

A parish-based process of evangelization and adult faith formation

Continue faith sharing in your small Christian communities after **ARISE Together in Christ** with ***WHY CATHOLIC? Journey through the Catechism.***

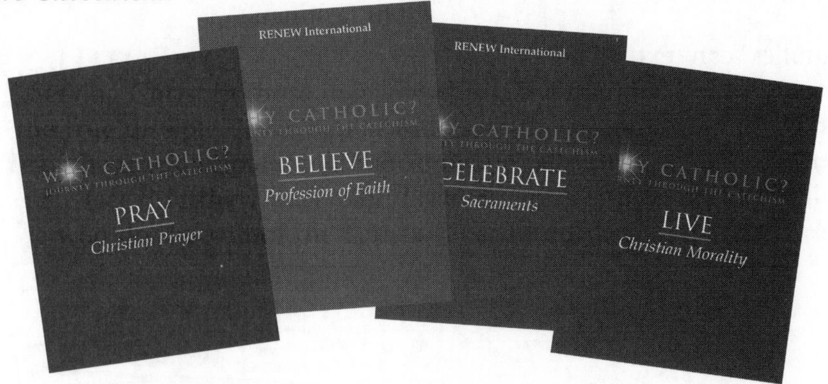

WHY CATHOLIC? Journey through the Catechism is a parish-based process of evangelization and adult faith formation from RENEW International. This process, designed for sharing in small Christian communities, is structured around exploring the important truths of our faith as they are presented in the *Catechism of the Catholic Church* and in the *United States Catholic Catechism for Adults.*

WHY CATHOLIC? helps nourish faith and enhance our sense of Catholic identity. The process and materials encourage us to understand and live the reasons why we are Catholic, and so lead us to a faith that is experienced more authentically, connecting us more deeply and meaningfully to God, and to others.

There are four books in the ***WHY CATHOLIC?*** series, each offering twelve sessions:

- **PRAY:** ***Christian Prayer***
- **BELIEVE:** ***Profession of Faith***
- **CELEBRATE:** ***Sacraments***
- **LIVE:** ***Christian Ministry***

For each of the four ***WHY CATHOLIC?*** books, there is a **Song CD**. Each CD is a 12-song compilation of the songs suggested for the moments of prayer during the faith-sharing sessions. The CDs are available singly, or as a set.

Families can extend the fruits of the sharing on the same themes presented in the books by using *RENEWing Family Faith*: attractive four-color companion bulletins with activities and reflections for sharing among different age groups.

WHY CATHOLIC? is far more than printed resources for faith-sharing in small communities. It is a complete integrated process providing materials and support both in print and on the web, together with opportunities for faith enrichment events and retreats for the whole parish, as well as a series of training workshops for small community leaders.

This process of faith-building through faith-sharing is also available in Spanish: ***¿POR QUÉ SER CATÓLICO?***

To learn more about bringing *WHY CATHOLIC? / ¿POR QUÉ SER CATÓLICO?* to your parish:

visit: www.whycatholic.org
email: whycatholic@renewintl.org
call: 908-769-5400